$\mathscr{P}$RAISE FOR
You Can Write a Romance

"Rita Clay Estrada is one of the most recognized names in the romance genre, not only for her fine writing ability but simply because she has given so much support and encouragement to so many writers, aspiring and published."
—Joan Hohl, aka Amii Loren, author of *Breeze Off the Ocean* and *Morgan Wade's Woman*

"No one is more qualified to write about romance than this mother-daughter team. Rita Gallagher's list of former students reads like a who's who of bestselling authors. And when I start reading one of Rita Clay Estrada's books, I know I won't put it down until reach the end."
—Constance O'Banyon, author of *Celebrations* and *Texas Proud*

"If you need to know anything about the business of romance writing, ask Rita Clay Estrada or Rita Gallagher."
—Mary Lynn Baxter, author of *Undercover Lovers* and *Autumn Awakening*

"An intelligent guide to romance written in clear, simple language to help with the labor of love you're about to undertake."
—Marie Ferrarella, author of *Cassandra* and *Cowboys Are for Loving*

"*You Can Write a Romance* is an invaluable guide to the writing and selling of a romance novel. I will enthusiastically recommend this book to my clients."
—Evan Marshall, New York literary agent

You Can Write a Romance

RITA CLAY ESTRADA AND
RITA GALLAGHER

WRITER'S DIGEST BOOKS
CINCINNATI, OHIO
www.writersdigest.com

Other fine Writer's Digest Books are available from your local bookstore or direct from the publisher.

Visit our Web site at www.writersdigest.com for information on more resources for writers.

To receive a free weekly E-mail newsletter delivering tips and updates about writing and about Writer's Digest products, send an E-mail with "Subscribe Newsletter" in the body of the message to newsletter-request@writersdigest.com, or register directly at our Web site at www.writersdigest.com.

03   02   01   00   99   5   4   3   2   1

Library of Congress Cataloging-in-Publication Data

Gallagher, Rita.
    You can write a romance / by Rita Gallagher and Rita Clay Estrada.—1st ed.
        p.   cm.
    Includes bibliographical references
    ISBN 0-89879-862-0 (alk. paper)
    1. Love stories—Authorship. 2. Love stories—Marketing. I. Estrada, Rita Clay. II. Title.
PN3377.5.L68G35   1999
808.3'85—dc21   99-14776
                                                                        CIP

Edited by Toni Herzog, Michelle Howry and Amanda Prenger
Cover photography by Brian Steege
Cover designed by Wendy Dunning

ACKNOWLEDGMENTS

We would like to thank those wonderful novelists who took the time to add their wit and wisdom to these pages. The pithy quotes scattered throughout this book are gifts—explaining in digestible spoonfuls of sugar, how the authors create the magic that holds readers to their stories. We thank them and we know that when you read this book, you will thank them, too.

Thank you Jack Heffron of Writer's Digest Books for suggesting this one. It was a labor—sometimes of love, sometimes of learning, but most often of hard work.

Thanks to Susan Shepherd, Harlequin Temptation editor, for her patience while completing this project. We appreciate her great sense of humor and help. Without her support this past year, it would have seemed an endless task.

And to beginning writers, please remember that there comes a time to read and a time to write. This is *reading* time. But as soon as you finish this book, it's *writing* time.

Good luck!
Rita Clay Estrada
Rita Gallagher

Rita Clay Estrada is creator, cofounder and first president of Romance Writers of America, the largest genre writing organization in the world. In early 1980, she sold her first book to Simon and Schuster. Since then she has published over thirty books with Silhouette, Dell, Leisure and Harlequin.

For more than four years, Rita acted as RWA spokeswoman on such programs as *CBS National News* with Steve Croft, the *Today Show*, *King TV* and *PBS National*, as well as many local television and radio shows. She has given workshops and been the keynote speaker at national conferences, universities and library systems throughout the country. She was listed in *Who's Who of American Women* in 1982, 1983 and 1984. In 1995, she was listed in *Two Thousand Notable American Women*.

Her books have won numerous awards and consistently make the national best-seller lists. The Romance Writers of America's annual published author awards were named the RITA in her honor.

Mainstream novelist and lecturer, Rita Gallagher and her daughter, Rita Clay Estrada, cofounded Romance Writers of America (RWA), the world's largest writers organization. Gallagher was first editor of RWA's monthly magazine, *The Romance Writer's Report*. In 1981 she coordinated the first RWA conference near Houston, Texas.

She is also a renowned novel structure teacher. Since she began teaching in 1982, more than two thousand books have been sold by her former students and more are hitting the book stands each month. In 1984 she opened Writer's Inspiration House, a haven for aspiring and published novelists where editors and agents joined in workshops and conferences for her students. Interviewed on local and national radio and television, featured in magazines and newspapers throughout the United States and Canada, she gives workshops at colleges and writer's conferences across the country.

Her fiction books brought fan mail worldwide, and *Writing Romances*, a Writer's Digest book coedited with her daughter, is in its second printing. *Structuring Your Novel*, her ninety-minute audio tape, was a Writer's Digest best-seller.

1 THE BASICS OF ROMANCE

A new writer has to face so many questions and such an overwhelming wealth of information that it sometimes becomes confusing.

Our own writing careers began before there was a network of writers to call upon. It took five times longer to find the answers we needed to get our manuscripts to the publishing houses in a form the editors were willing to read, judge and perhaps buy. Although there was scant information, in other ways it was easier because we weren't bombarded with too much "stuff."

Any given year, forty percent *or more* of all fiction books sold are romances. That makes the publishing industry competitive and the reading market a sophisticated, hungry tiger. How wonderful when things balance out like that!

We hope this book will answer those hundreds of questions that plagued us as beginning writers, and give a chance to a manuscript that is well written and ready to buy. Many questions we've heard at writers conferences have to do with what happens after a writer completes and successfully sells a romance. What can she expect to happen? What about payments? Galleys? Royalties? Editing? Publication dates? Assigned editors? Proof of research? All of these questions are valid, and we hope to answer every one. We remember asking the same questions, and the kind writers who took time from their own careers to answer them. To them, we will forever be thankful. Because of them, we will be able to answer those same questions for you. However, the answers aren't necessary for you to write a good book. Remember that, please.

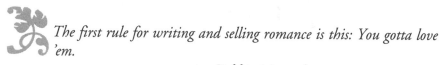

The first rule for writing and selling romance is this: You gotta love 'em.
                                        —Debbie Macomber

What Is Romance?

Let's start from the beginning. What is a romance? With all the books out there, why is one called a *romance* while another is labeled *women's fiction* or *western* or *science fiction* or *mystery* or *techno-thriller* or . . . well, you get the point.

It's so simple, and so very complicated. A romance is present in every book that has a man and woman falling in love, but all of those books are not part of the romance genre. A story is only a romance when the main theme of that book is romance!

In other words, it doesn't matter whether it's a western, mystery or science fiction as long as the main theme is romance. Then, and only then, can it be called a romance.

The expanding marketplace for romances has allowed the genre to evolve into formula fiction without the formula.
                                        —Debbie Macomber

What Is Not a Romance?

If the main theme of a story is a man and woman fighting for their lives against the Mafia as they fall in love with each other, it's probably a thriller. If the man and woman fight *each other* as they try to flee the Mafia, it's probably a romance.

See the difference?

Whatever the emphasis is, that's what the book is. Think of movies: *Star Wars* was a science fiction story with a romance growing between the action. *Pretty Woman* was a romance set in the powerful elite of the corporate world. The basic rule is that for a book to be a romance, the romance must be the most important element in the story.

Now to throw in a monkey wrench.

Danielle Steel–types of books aren't romances. They're known as *soaps*. Why? Because they're problematic—one heart-kicking dilemma after another. One life-threatening quandary after another. One tear-jerking, emotional death and divorce after another. The romance is secondary to the problems, growth and tears of the heroine. That's a soap. Danielle Steele created the written form and made it her genre. Many have followed, but few have had the success she has.

Maeve Binchy and others have created another genre . . . and you guessed it, these books are not romances either. This genre deals with women—the problems and quiet realities of their lives. These women experience growth, new beginnings, raising children alone and doing it to the best of their ability, leaving husbands and winning the economic war, going back to school, opening businesses and going to work for the first time. Through all of this, they make a success of their lives. This genre is called *women's fiction*.

In an equal, more knowledgeable world, this would all be called just good plain fiction. It used to be, but not now.

The publishing industry has an odd view of fiction sales. If you took away genre and subgenre fictions, what would you have? You'd have what the market supports today: general fiction and women's fiction. The reasoning is that general fiction is anything written by a male that both men and women read. Women's fiction can be written by men or women, but is usually aimed at women, since most American men don't (yes, you may read "won't" here) read women fiction writers unless it's in a genre they can publicly relate to—a genre like mystery (Sue Grafton, Agatha Christie, Mary Higgins Clark, etc.).

All methods of writing (including those in this book) can be applied to any type of fiction writing. Good plot and good writing span all kinds of storytelling. However, this book is aimed at romance fiction.

We hope we can explain all about the romance genre by starting at the heart of romance. And that place is called *category romance*, a good place to study the genre in a form that's pure.

Category—The Heart of Romance

Category books are produced in *lines*. Lines come out with new titles monthly, and a set amount of books are usually published each month. All books in a line carry the same theme. They also have a set word count and topic, and each line has a very personal tone. Each line is different, although sometimes the differences are subtle. Any books published in the Harlequin lines (Temptation, American, Presents, Romance, etc.) or Silhouette lines (Desire, Romance, Intimate Moments, etc.) are category books. Also, almost all category lines are contemporary romances, and most have word counts of 75,000 words or less. Therefore, category romance is often referred to as "short contemporary" romance.

Categories are very important for the romance genre. They not only have very loyal fans, but they introduce new trends in fiction that are exploding or sneaking in the back door. What you see now in the microcosm of category romance, you can bet you'll see in stand-alone books in the near future.

Any story where the main theme is love between a man and a woman is a romance.

Basic Plot of Romance

In a romance, there is One True Love for the heroine, and once he comes on the scene early in the book, there are no other men for her—just as, from that point, there are no other women for him (especially in category romances). The hero doesn't cheat on the heroine, and although there are times he may want to throttle her, he never, ever lays a hand on her. That's the basic backdrop for the plot.

For every rule we've just stated, you can find an exception in the nearest bookstore. However, those writers have already sold their work. The very word, *exception*, tells you how hard it would be to sell an out-of-the-mainstream story as your first book. Stay in the middle of the road and write mainstream stories until you sell. Then, when you have a book or two under your belt and your editor wants another, you can try something out of the ordinary. It's easier to slip a foot in the publishing door when it doesn't have a ten-ton ball and chain attached.

Now, when we say middle-of-the-road story, we certainly don't mean middle-of-the-road characters. They need to be original and spicy, with distinct personalities. Characterization is where you can get creative and really show your style.

Let's face it. You need two main things to write a good story: a tight plot, and realistic characters who live on after the book is put down. It can be 60–40 or 40–60, but it's best when it's 100–100.

By the way, a lot of good published stories have had better characters than plots, but no one cared because the characters *were* so good that the reader suspended disbelief.

A Romance Novel Is . . .

- about a woman trying to achieve her heart's desire, facing and fighting obstacles to reach it—and succeeding in the end.
- about a woman learning who she is, finding her place in the world, then fighting to gain (or keep) it.
- about the uncertain and confusing feelings that go with that most important part of women's emotions—*love!*
- about the irresistible physical and emotional attraction between male and female. Some lines (like Harlequin Romance or Steeple Hill) deal subtly with this aspect of romance. Others, like Harlequin Temptation and Silhouette Desire are more descriptive about sexual attraction—and about sex. However, whether subtle or descriptive, romance with all its joys and many-faceted complications is what makes the world go around.

My first editor, Vivian Stephens, once told me, "When you get the world's attention, you'd better have something good to say." That has stuck with me to this day, twenty years later. A writer's priority must be the book. Invariably, other publishing idiosyncrasies—poor distribution, lousy covers, sloppy editing, promotion or the lack thereof, scathing reviews—become distracting factors. But the writer's primary focus must forever and always be the manuscript. If it's not good, nothing else matters.
—Sandra Brown

A romance novel, like any other kind of book, should have a *wow* start, something that instantly pulls the reader into the story. The first sentence should make the reader care about what's going to happen, and curious enough to race through the pages to satisfy that curiosity.

From Root Ideas to Character Growth

The past pages give a general idea of what a romance novel is all about. Now let's go a little deeper. What follows is an overview of what it takes to actually write a romance novel.

Writing a Story With Purpose

The first thing to think about is: What is my story about? *Theme. Root idea. Premise.* What do those words mean? They mean there must be a reason or purpose for your story. If you know what you're trying to prove when you write your romance novel, the words will flow easier, your characters will respond better and the entire design of the book will fall into place. Are you trying to prove that a woman who once loved and lost can love again? Or that a woman who loves her own child enough to kidnap her isn't really a criminal?

No matter what your purpose, jump into the middle of the problem. Then, after briefly sketching the back story, show step by step why (as in the first example) a woman *can* love again. Or why the kidnapping mom *isn't* a criminal.

As you proceed don't forget that this is a *romance* novel. The hero must be introduced almost immediately, and he should complicate things for the heroine, not make them easier. Ultimately, the heroine has to solve her problems for herself and reconcile her attraction to this man who is making her goal more difficult. Because love, though sometimes difficult, is balanced with joy, during your story your character's perspective will change; she will be able to resolve her problem on her own, strengthened by the hero's love.

How she responds to this change in her life—how, because of love, her focus changes, converges, then tries to readjust—is the heart of your story.

Premise Is the First Step to Plotting

The plot is the map or the blueprint of your book. Knowing your premise and sticking to it will keep your story from losing energy and direction. Premise will keep your story on what editors call "the main thrust" and help each step, incident and reaction evolve logically. Although the reader doesn't know where you're heading, you need to know at all times. Sometimes that's easier said than done, like when you're in the middle of a great scene and the dialogue gets away from you, but it's worth the effort in a well-plotted story.

The Rules of Sexual Awareness/Tension

A romance novel has two more important ingredients:
- sexual awareness
- sexual tension

Rule One: From the first time they meet, the hero and heroine are deeply aware of each other. They don't have to like each other instantly, but they do have to be aware. This awareness escalates, changes and rearranges throughout the story and culminates in the resolution.

Rule Two: The hero and heroine should be together as much as possible. In scenes where they are necessarily apart, the absent one should be kept in the reader's mind through memories, yearnings, etc.

Rule Three: Each time they are together, their feelings should take on another aspect. Their emotions will strengthen, shake, threaten—and as the book progresses—solidify the relationship.

Rule Four: The senses of hero and heroine are sharpened when they are together. Whether they are fighting or on the verge of making love, sexual tension escalates with each scene.

Conflict

A woman betrayed by love decides to give up all men for the rest of her life. Then, having charted her course, she is suddenly confronted with the hero, who shatters all her previous conceptions about the opposite sex. Both inner and outer conflict will appear here. And again, senses, feelings and emotions are the three parts of the engine propelling the story to a satisfactory conclusion.

Conflict is the engine that moves the story forward. There is no story without it. Conflict forces the characters to modify their different traits and perspectives. It forces the hero and heroine to rise above the situation, become strong, find themselves and their self-esteem. In a romance, just like in any other well-written novel, conflict is the crux of the story.

A romance novel is about two very different people who meet and, despite differing perspectives, fall in love. Throughout the book, they overcome their differences, learn from each other and, in the process, draw closer together.

A romance novel is about two halves becoming a whole—then joining forces to become two joined wholes. (This is our personal philosophy, but history has proven that every well-received book holds the same premise.)

Why? Because one of the things we've learned over the years is that the best romance novels are not about codependence; they are about finding love in equality. The female has problems to work out and a

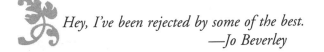

Hey, I've been rejected by some of the best.
—Jo Beverley

process to learn from. She will make him fall in love with her and help teach him his own lesson. Now that's a *woman*—not a dainty flower or a codependent wimp who can't live without a man to guide her!

That is one of the most important points we can make to you. These female characters are stronger than they know, more inventive than they give themselves credit for and are number one survivors. The man is the extra. He is not the only way to go.

And we don't believe that one character flaw should be used to illustrate the fullness of true love. It's not the right image to demonstrate in this form of print. We said image because we think romances help strengthen minds and resolves, defining what is right and good about men *and* women!

Characters Make the Conflict

Before writing about your characters, get to know them. Give them opposite backgrounds, personalities and traits.

Example: A fragile, gentle woman owns a china shop. She falls in love with a muscle-bound, former football player who doesn't know Limoges from Wedgewood. Each time he enters the shop he creates disaster. But when he takes her in his arms for a passionate kiss, she is treated like rare porcelain.

He is a hamburger and beer man; she is a caviar and champagne lady. *Result—conflict!*

She loves the symphony and ballet; he finds them terribly boring. She loves attending theater parties on opening night; he hates to wear a tux. In every aspect of her life (except for her choice in a man), she is rigidly formal.

Result—conflict!

What does he have to learn from her?

What does she have to learn from him?

If you know the personality of the heroine and hero, you will know which traits will draw them together and which traits will create conflict between them.

With some skill and thought, you can even turn these character tags around and still have a strong story.

Expressing Character Through Point of View

Point of view (POV) is the person who's telling the story. If it's the female, then you're writing as if you're in her head, thinking her thoughts and feeling her desires, needs and wants. You do the same thing if it's the male point of view.

A long time ago, writers (especially new writers) were told to stay in one viewpoint forever: the female point of view. Now editors and readers alike want to see both sides of the main characters.

Note: That does not mean that you skip from one head to another to another and then back again. For reader identification and ease, stay in one mind for each scene.

Because women relate best to basic female emotions, the heroine's viewpoint is usually presented. Every woman understands the pain of lost love or betrayal, whether or not she has experienced it. Women also understand the determination to seek a goal and the joy of achieving it, regardless if the goal is fame, fortune or a man.

In a romance novel, another key word is *man.* If a woman thinks that all she wants is fame, fortune and a career, a man will usually pop up to complicate her life and give her more than she bargained for. That's what a romance novel is all about: Goal (whatever she wants or strives for) = achievement and love.

Now let's talk about the male point of view.

Writing is an action verb. Do it, don't just talk about it.
—Marie Ferrarella

What is important about the hero? The hero is the catalyst for the heroine. Like a powerful magnet, he enters her life and creates physical and emotional chaos. (So what's the difference in real life? Not much!) The heroine is drawn to him, and all her prior ideas about life and love are turned topsy-turvy. How she deals with this hero and her own private, conflicting emotions are what the story is all about.

There is another reason for explaining the thought processes of the hero in a romance novel. Within those pages, a reader finds the hero of her dreams: the man that she married or wants to marry. Not that he's perfect—he can't be perfect, and neither can the heroine. But the interaction and growth they experience, no matter how abrasive at the beginning, brings out the best in each of them by the story's end.

The greatest joy women find in the hero's role is seeing what makes him tick. For years men were seen as gods, strong and virile. They ruled the woman's world and many were intimidated by their power. In a

9

romance novel, the reader is given a peek inside those Lords of the Realm. Many female souls rejoice when they see that men are also vulnerable. Men can be hurt, they can yearn, suffer and even cry. And miracle of miracles, when true love takes over a man's heart, he can change. He can grow and become as strong as the women we admire. The heroine he loves can smooth his rough edges. She can teach tenderness where there was insensitivity, compassion where there was heartlessness, and selflessness where there was selfishness. She can show him the strength in being vulnerable. And the reader identifies.

Romance heroines aren't "women who love too much," nor are they perfect. They tackle their problems head-on and stand by their convictions. These are women of courage, risk-takers. Women as real as you and me.

—Debbie Macomber

Prevailing Over Conflict

By their very natures, your characters create story energy through conflict.

What she wants isn't what he wants.

What he thinks isn't what she thinks.

He disagrees with what she does and vice versa.

With all that conflict, what, you ask, could possibly hold these two people together?

Answer: These five points:

1. A strong physical (chemical) attraction
2. The fact that opposites attract
3. The hero's surprise to find a woman who isn't so blinded by his charm that she keeps her opinions to herself
4. Or, though intrigued by the hero, the heroine fights being told what to do, when to do it, how to think, etc.
5. Committed love! All the push/pull of likes, dislikes, fights and make-ups forces both hero and heroine to look, not only at each other but at themselves.

Because the heroine is a strong and worthy adversary, the hero grows strong and worthy, too. You can also reverse the theory, but we like it this way best.

What do these five points accomplish? Character growth.

What Is Character Growth?

With every painful hit life hands us, we adjust and grow, change our perspective and try to avoid making that same hurtful mistake again; if you realize this, then you already know about character growth.

While we create, experience and live with our characters, we may forget that with each impact, each mood swing, each reaction to the hits along the road to the character's goal, that character is changing. We also change as we react to life's lessons through our own personal disasters. With each problem, we change our perspective, our methods of coping, and we find new means to reach our goals. There isn't a time when we aren't constantly shifting to meet whatever specific goal we have set.

The same thing applies to your characters. A book is a slice of life, and real, live characters react in the same way as real, live people.

Many times when a hopeful author finishes or nearly finishes a book, the vital point of character growth has been overlooked.

Keep in mind that your characters will never again be the same as they were at the beginning of the story. Their story lives will force them to change and grow.

Giving Your Characters Goals and Motivations

Just like you, if a character has a strong goal, she is strongly motivated to reach it.

Ask yourself these questions:

1. Are your main characters goal oriented?
2. Do they have the inner strength, motivation and persistence to fight for their goals?

Note: Perhaps at the beginning of the story, the two main characters have very different goals. But as they interact through conflict and disasters, they are drawn together and in the end, achieve happiness with just a slight modification of their original goals—because of character growth.

3. Remembering that a reader doesn't want to enter weak, insipid characters, have you shown enough *present* strength and potential in your hero/heroine for them to grow and, through constant striving, achieve their goals?
4. As your characters progress and persist, are they taking honorable

chances that will make them grow and try new things despite whatever obstacles they encounter?

5. Have you stayed away from the old and tired "victim of fate"? Remember, readers want ever-strengthening characters getting a handle on life while focusing on cherished goals.

We hope these brief "encounters" about the ingredients of romance novelwriting have piqued your interest enough to make you read further. In the following chapters, you will find more in-depth information about the lessons touched upon here.

Meanwhile, what are you supposed to do to keep your writing alive and well?

Read, Read, Read

Read everything and anything that piques your interest. Read fiction from the best-seller list. (*Whose* best-seller list is up to you. The order will be different, but all the lists will carry most of the same books.)

Read anything and everything from your general genre. Category romance? Read a couple from each category, then go back and read a couple more from each category. Get a good, overall flavor of the various lines and how they speak to different topics. This is one way to learn who you like most, what publisher you want to write for, and what the guidelines are that set up each line.

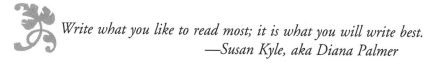

Write what you like to read most; it is what you will write best.
    —*Susan Kyle, aka Diana Palmer*

Read nonfiction, any type you like: bios, poetry, narrative prose, do-it-yourself books, westerns, spy stories, classics that weren't introduced to you in school. . . in other words, the entire gamut.

Read anything that will educate you on living. On becoming better at anything. On writing.

The most important research you can do is read. Read everything, especially the category in which you want to write. Every writer I know is an avid reader. Reading is the first love; then writing comes naturally.
    —*Mary Tate, aka Tate McKenna*

The point is that all books will be of some value to you and your writing. Maybe it won't benefit the book you're working on right this minute, but it might for the book that you do next, or next after that, or next after that. Every piece of information is something you'll use down the line.

Reading everything from cereal boxes to billboards will help you learn more about writing than anything else you can do for yourself. It will keep your mind active, keep you interested in writing and help you learn to recognize and fix your mistakes.

And yes, you will make mistakes. Why? If you're not making mistakes, you're not writing. Just like life. It's as simple as that.

2 DIFFERENCES IN ROMANCE NOVELS

As soon as this book is published, someone will say, "You forgot subgenre X!" And they'll be right, because it seems the number of romance subgenres grows every day. Some of these subgenres may surprise you. Paranormal? Medieval? Suspense? Yes, they can also be romances if the focus is on the relationship.

One of the authors of this book, Rita Clay Estrada, wrote a romance called *The Ivory Key*, which took more than eight years to get published. At the time it was completed, it didn't fit neatly into any existing subgenre. The hero was an eighteenth-century ghost, and the book had history, contemporary politics, paranormal elements and suspense all wrapped up into one story. But it really didn't matter what subgenre it was because, first and foremost, it was a romance.

Rita also wrote about an alien from another world who came down to earth, shape-shifted into a dead spouse and collected babies in liquid form. Guess what? It's a romance! She named it *Forms*, and the publisher renamed it *Forms of Love*. It was science fiction dressed in today's world. First and foremost, it was a romance.

If you remember the basic rules for romances, historical or contemporary, you will know what each very similar or exceedingly different story needs to be included in that genre. After that, do what you want to make it the best, most interesting story you can possibly write.

Now that we've established the difference between a romance and any other fiction, let's talk about some of the basic differences between one romance and another.

There is no perfect time to write. Something always comes up to eat your free time. Instead, take an hour here, a half hour there, a moment here. It will eventually add up to a complete story told—and sold.
—Parris Afton Bonds

Category Romance

We already know what the average category romance is from the definition in chapter one. It's the 55,000- to 90,000-word book that comes out in a line, so many per month (usually two, four or six), with the publishing house logo printed as importantly as the average writer's name. Because of its size, its main thrust must be romance first, characters second, then any other additional elements.

The following is a list of the most common types of category romances:

The Sweet Romance: A romance that contains sensuality without sexuality; technically, there is no sex before marriage. Christian romances fall into this category.

The Intrigue: This romance is surrounded by danger and mystery and often contains a "woman in jeopardy."

The Sensual Romance: This romance contains sensuality *and* sexuality; but remember, the characters are still monogamous and in love. Otherwise, it wouldn't be a romance.

The Romantic Comedy: A romance that incorporates humor and takes on a lighthearted tone.

The Mainstream Category: This probably seems like a contradiction, but a mainstream romance takes on the best of both worlds. It is written in the personal tone of the line it's in, but it is a longer book than other category novels. It explores issues and emotions on a deeper level.

Try to have no more than eight characters and one subplot in a category romance. Generally, write between eight and fourteen chapters, and keep the word count evenly spaced among the chapters.

15

Blank screen, blank mind? Ideas for plots can be found in Shakespeare, the Bible, history texts, newspapers, opera stories, children's books, television, magazines, gossip, rumors—even in your neighbor's rambling stories. Modernize, change and twist them to make them your own. Think of those fictional novels based on or inspired by a real-life event!
—*Jane Tun*

Mainstream Romance

A mainstream romance (also called "single-title romance" or "long contemporary romance") is basically a stand-alone book. Since it isn't in a series, it can come out whenever the publisher chooses. Although there is no specific word count, the mainstream romance is usually around 90,000 to 125,000 words. This is an average word count publishers use to give you something to shoot for. No house or editor has ever turned down a great stand-alone romance—or any other book for that matter—because its word count was too little or too much. Turning down a book usually means it is not the content the publisher/editor is interested in or wants to work to improve.

Because this type of novel has a larger size, it can have far more characters than are possible in a category book. All kinds of things can be going on: several subplots, subcharacters, more texture, more travel, character development. You name it, you can have it—as long as you remember that the main theme is romance!

Historicals

Romance publishing has its own definition of a historical novel. According to the powers that be (the publishing houses), the historical novel can begin in 1066—when William the Conqueror and the Normans defeated the Saxons of Great Britain—and end as late as 1899, a time distant enough to be considered "historical" by the masses.

Within the historical genre are two categories. Anything from 1066 to just beyond 1500 is a *medieval romance*, because it will generally contain some of the following elements:
- knights
- honor and chivalry
- the French and English at war
- castles and keeps
- herbs and midwives

Anything from around 1500 to 1899 is simply considered a *historical romance* and will contain elements appropriate to the year or years in which it is set. Historical romances are mainly stand-alone novels, similar to mainstream romances. However, historical romance is a large genre of its own and has spawned several subgenres.

Regencies

The *Regency novel* deserves a special mention among historicals, since in many ways it is a category novel within a single-title genre. The Regency market is also one that never seems to waver. Ask an independent bookstore owner, and he will tell you Regency novels have an intensely loyal readership that enjoys "the romp."

The Regency period was a specific time in history: 1811 to 1820, give or take a few years. It was a time when Napoleon was pillaging Europe. England secretly drooled over France's cognac and silks, finally going to war to get them. English society was firmly divided between upper and lower classes, and marriages, especially among the nobility, were still arranged. Women struggled with issues of inequality (men were "expected" to take mistresses, while women were lumped into one of two categories: ladies or whores), and *everyone* struggled to maintain the rigid standards of "polite society."

Jane Austen lived in this time period and wrote what are often considered the first Regency romance novels, only for her they were contemporary romances. Georgette Heyer is a master of the Regency genre, with fast pacing, great subtleties and witty dialogue.

Some Regency writers have left category regencies behind for the larger, mainstream Regency story (commonly called a Regency period historical as opposed to "a Regency"). There they can create dark, mysterious plots, delineate characters into shades of gray rather than just good and evil, and have—gasp!—love scenes that are more than just a kiss and a grope, which is taboo in a regular regency. They can forage among all the facts and fallacies of the day, exposing the underbelly of society while exploring the personal lives of the men and women of that time.

I say: Quite wonderful, by Jove.

What Is Not a Historical Romance

Period Novels: Books written about the years from 1900 to the present are called *period novels.* We know it seems that this is historical too, but most publishing houses consider the 1900s too recent to be called historical. It also bears mentioning that a romance set in this period is generally very difficult (although not impossible) to sell.

Sagas: These long, mainstream books are often family stories, although they can be friend stories, house stories, business stories, etc. They have a central thread held through several generations, beginning with a patriarch/matriarch passing down land, money, opportunity or some other kind of legacy to the next generation. Some kind of conflict thus ensues, which is then perpetuated generation after generation.

Usually, sagas cover three generations, occasionally four. The book's theme—its central thread or spine—holds and molds story and characters. It's strong. It's family, whether factual or fictionalized. The story carries on the original conflict until, at last, it is resolved by the present generation.

In short, think of the building and financial empire of Joseph Kennedy to JFK to John-John, or the legacies of the Vanderbilt women for the past three generations.

Interesting? You bet. Still, a saga, though including romance, usually does not fall under the romance genre.

It's a terrific read, but unless you're a natural, it's not an easy book to write. Sagas are not three different stories of three different women who happen to be related; all threads must tie each generation together. It's three women usually on the same mission or seeking the same thing. Sagas depict a wide scope of growth for females. Lost or unrequited love is a perfect background for lessons learned and wisdom acquired to pass on to the next generation of women.

Westerns: This type of book is anything set in the 1800s in the western United States. Westerns will consist of pioneers, cowboys, gunfights, hangings, cattle, sheep and women trying to make it alone. Romances can, and often are, set in the West during this period; as we've said, it's a matter of balance and focus. If more time is spent on gunfights than romance, it's a western; if the gunfights and all else revolve around the romance, then it's a romance. (This is made all the more confusing by the fact that when romance writers talk about writing romances set in the West, they often call them "westerns" for brevity's sake.)

Civil War Books: These books can be from the perspective of the North or South and can take place just before, during, or after the Civil War. The events and emotions within the story will be influenced by the war. Can it be a romance? The same rules apply here as with any other book. If it focuses on battles and loyalty and societal issues, it is a Civil War book. But if all those elements revolve around two people in love, you have a romance.

The inspirational romance, one of the fastest growing markets in recent years, adds a third element to the usual external (action) and internal (emotion) plots. That element is the spiritual plot, used to reveal how the hero's and heroine's relationships with God affect their relationship with each other.
—Robin Lee Hatcher

Christian Romances

Christian romances are sold primarily in Christian bookstores and privately owned grocery stores, but they are a growing market that can be found with increasing frequency in bookstores and other large chain stores. The theme is still romance, but with a slightly different slant. There is little sex, but certainly sensuality, and in the end, the heroine always converts the hero to her way of thinking.

The Christian market also contains historicals, sagas and category novels. In fact, many of the Silhouette Romances were "converted" to this market by some rewriting.

Don't let the name "Christian" fool you. This market is as well written and interesting as any other, but you need to research it and read, read, read it to pinpoint its subtle differences.

No matter how many novels an author has published in paperback, she will feel like a beginner when the publisher decides to debut her in hardback. A whole new set of pressures suddenly appear on the horizon. It sometimes helps to know it is like that for others besides oneself.
—Robin Lee Hatcher

Paperback vs. Hardback

We've all seen them: Star authors who go from paperback to hardback, their names splashed all over the dust jacket. And how impressive to actually have a jacket to keep the dust off the books! The current high prices of books loudly proclaim they're making tons of money. And a year after its release in hardback, the same story will come out in paperback and hit every best-seller list *again*.

It's one of those mixed blessings. You're so jealous you could spit glue, and you're so proud they made it in a genre you love that you could carry the book around forever in every airport and restaurant you visit.

Be aware that most writers who make it that far worked for the privilege, sweated blood for it, honed their talent to a fine edge and earned it by paying dues, both private and public, that we'll probably never know about, but respect anyway.

Recently, the publishers have created a new sort of hardback: a hardback cover the size of a paperback. The paper is pure and white and expensive and will probably outlive our great-great-grandchildren long into the next millennium.

If a hardback is your goal, follow what those writers have done and it could happen to you, too. But remember one thing: Every one of those authors always wrote the best story they could. That goal was first and foremost on their minds. Rest assured that it was the storytelling, the craftsmanship and the persistence that got them into hardcover.

> *One half of selling a novel is simply to work steadily; the other half is composed of skill, style and luck.*
> —Anne Marie Winston

Your job as a writer, should you choose to accept it, is to tell the best story you can, honing the ability you have. No less.

Writing a big, single-title romance (contemporary or historical) or a smaller category novel takes a lot of preparation. That preparation cost is high—in time, thought and research. The old saying is true: Anything worth doing is worth doing well.

3 THE BUSINESS SIDE OF ROMANCE

If you hang out in bookstores, studying books, authors and sales treatments, you've probably recognized a particular trend lately: A dozen or so publishing houses use several imprint names that belong to the same house. Over the past twenty years, I've watched large publishers gulp down smaller publishers, one corporation after another.

So when you're sitting in your home and writing your heart out, don't feel that you're a little cottage industry pecking away. You're not.

You're a cog in the wheel of a very large corporation whose essence is to have a good bottom line; stock will sell, shareholders will be happy and jobs will increase; publicity money will grease the wheels of the economy so warehouses can be filled with books; distributors can move orders to bookstores so they can pay all their part-time workers (except for the manager, who is much like slave labor, filling in wherever there is a breach in the time sheets); and customers can have their choice of reading Book A, Book B and Book C, ad infinitum.

It's the trickle-down theory. For the most part, and if you're into politics, it *might* work. In fact, since that's the way business is already set up, we hope it works!

But, being very large and cumbersome, publishing corporations occasionally get leery of trying anything different unless it's a well-known author. They rely on the editor's word; for the most part, the corporate structure doesn't read every book to come down the pike. Far from it.

What does that mean for you? Well, let's just say Stephen King can write any darn thing he wants; you can't.

Follow Your Book Through the Publishing House

If an unagented manuscript is sent to a publishing house, but not addressed to a specific editor, it goes into the *slush pile*. It is sometimes returned unread if the author included postage. Thousands of unagented manuscripts are sent to publishers each month, and busy editors don't have time to read them all. Requested manuscripts from published authors are usually read first. Agented manuscripts are read next because the agent vouches for the work. Also, as we will discuss later, the agent knows the type of book that particular publisher accepts, so the manuscript has a better chance of reaching publication.

Meet the Editors

Editors work for the publishing corporations. Generally, several editors work under each imprint line, which is the second name of the publishing house.

Your editor is your partner, not your enemy. You have the same goal: A best-selling, award-winning book that reflects well on both of you. The fine art of compromise is as important to publishing as basic grammar skills are to writing.

—Gina Wilkins

Harlequin Temptation or Silhouette Intimate Moments are examples of imprints.

Editors come with their own chain of command: editor in chief, senior editor, editor, assistant editor. Each of these titles indicates a step up the ladder and is very important as far as power, experience, salary, acquisitions, author stable and a lot of other stuff we know little or nothing about. Editors come in all sizes and sexes (just like real people!), but for romance and women's fiction genres, they're usually female. Editors buy your story, help keep your plot on target, make sure the characters you created remain true to themselves, and ensure that the combination hangs together while keeping the reader's interest. Editors help you keep the same tone through the entire manuscript. They write you long letters explaining what needs to be done to make it a more marketable book. They also choose the inside blurb on your book that makes the characters sparkle and creates interest; then they write the back blurb that will pique everyone's appetites. They will write the *teaser*, the blurb put in someone else's book to advertise yours in advance of publication. All this, and then your editor will heap praise upon you when it's done. Good editors don't let you know they just gave a tired sigh of relief themselves.

When it comes to working with an editor, don't sweat the small stuff. You're much more likely to win when it really matters to you if you don't challenge every editorial suggestion.
　　　　　　　　　　　　　　—Gina Wilkins

Believe us when we say a good editor is worth gold and a bad editor is . . . still worth something. If nothing else, she may teach you to stand up for your work or force you to move on to another house. (In our estimation, moving to another publishing house to leave an editor behind has happened more often than any other reason for moving, including larger advances.)

An editor is at times overwhelmed with work from her stable of published authors—authors who have proven themselves, who have a readership and whose books routinely reach the bookstores.

Editors read optioned material (manuscripts that have been requested on previous contracts), revised manuscripts and best-sellers looking for a new home. Phone calls and meetings are also part of a busy editor's day.

Standing as backup to editors are the *copyeditors*, who check grammar problems, factoids and the occasional slips in time lines, if necessary. They read and they double check.

Then come secretaries. Even these employees read, read, read. They are informative, enthusiastic and have great insight into the story and its problems. They often take home manuscripts to read and know the schedule on the board better than others in the office. Some are working their way up to being editors, while others just enjoy the extra work because they're readers at heart.

What Happens to an Eye-Catching Manuscript?
So, is all this necessary for a good book? After all, aren't your sterling words alone strong enough to sell that baby? You're a good writer!

23

Some of the best tips I received as a beginning writer came from rejections letters, which can be invaluable learning tools. Friends and critique groups won't necessarily be brutally honest about your work. Editors will. Learn from them.

—*Gina Wilkins*

If your golden, written-in-stone-and-uncorrected words were all that was needed to put your story on the bookstore shelf, you could bet major bucks that sales would not exceed whatever your family and friends would buy.

And since there are other books vying for the sound of the cashier's ring, you'd better have something outstanding to catch a reader's eye instantly—like an eye-catching cover, a great back blurb, a tightness in style and a story line that captures the reader's imagination. All of those items are sales tools to get the reader where we (writers) want them. Where is that? Opening the book to the *piece de resistance* . . . a great, knock-your-socks-off first page. But the first eyes you have to catch are those of the various readers and editors we've just discussed.

If the editor in a larger publishing house is persuaded by the cover letter, and a partial or complete manuscript is sent, an in-house reader will read it and give a report. The report usually boils down to a few paragraphs giving plot description and the reader's opinion. Many manuscripts will receive no further attention.

However, if the reader recommends the manuscript, the editor will look at it. If the editor doesn't like it, it will be returned to the author.

In order for the magic to happen, you have to be there. That means planting yourself religiously in front of your computer and working. If you write it, it will come.

—*Marie Ferrarella*

If the work passes the editor's muster, it will be presented at the editorial meeting, or another editor will be asked to give it a second read. If it passes that editor's scrutiny, the editor must then convince the editor in chief, the publisher, the sales department and (depending upon the book) the publicity department.

The editorial meeting is comprised of a group of professionals who must be convinced that the book is worthy of the time and resources of the publishing company. If it passes that meeting, then a *profit-and-loss estimate* is done—a projection of what the book will cost in acquiring, producing and publishing the finished product. It's a guesstimate of the point at which a book pays off and the rest of the income becomes profit. Then and only then is a decision made by publisher and editor about whether to buy the book.

If They Buy the Book

If the book is deemed worthy of being bought, the author is offered an advance. If accepted, she receives a contract and upon returning the contract with her signature, the agreed-upon advance. If revisions are necessary, the advance will be halved and the balance will be received when revisions are satisfactorily completed.

There are no shortcuts to a sale. You have to be willing to sacrifice a lot of free time while you're breaking into the field, and you have to learn to take rejection, because very rarely does a first novel sell. This is the hardest thing of all—you have to be persistent and keep those manuscripts in the mail, even when your ego is even with your socks. There might be a sale right around the next corner, so you have to keep going even when you don't feel like it.

—Susan Kyle aka Diana Palmer

From then on, the book is out of the writer's hands (who hopefully is already writing another) and into the editor's capable hands. The procedure then goes like this:

- A publication date is scheduled.
- A copyeditor checks for grammar, style and punctuation, as well as checking information for validity. This may include wanting to know where the author acquired certain dates or incidents in a historical, as well as pointing out that it never snows in south Texas or that orange trees do not grow in Iowa.

The Marketing Department

The marketing department is in charge of sales and distribution and usually has more men than women. Their general opinion is used for book covers and titles, as well as which writers are selling and what general comments are about the line, the book, the writer. That doesn't mean they read everything; they don't.

25

Most of the time, they're right on the money. Sometimes they're not.

Many a writer has heard the phrase, "Marketing didn't think your title would sell so they've chosen another," or "Marketing didn't think that story idea would fly." Sometimes their choice or idea is much better. Sometimes it's much worse.

As a first-time author, remember that publishing employees are all trying to sell the book. They don't purposely come up with off-the-wall, no-good titles or art or ideas. Everyone is interested in getting the product out there and making the best possible sale. During times of trial, keep that thought in mind.

The Art Department

Cover-art departments are another world. They don't read the books to figure out how to design the covers. They have cover art sheets that are filled out with the statistics of the characters and story line (hair color, eyes, height, weight, location, landmarks, etc.).

The art department hires photographers to shoot covers. Then, many are painted from the photos. They have a different time slot than the book does—the cover must usually be completed before the book is ready for galleys (which is the test printing of your manuscript).

When it is approved, the finished art is presented and may need further approval. Then the manuscript, synopsis and other pertinent material go to the copy department for jacket copy. Your name and the book's title are added to the cover art last.

Sometimes the colors are lost when covers are mass produced. For instance, a redhead may turn out a brunette, a blond may become a redhead—all from the inks changing. It's not done intentionally—it just happens. Cover colors aren't an exact science yet, especially when printers are producing so many. (It's amazing we can identify five hundred-year-old dead people by DNA chemistry, but we can't seem to accomplish this.) However, as the writer of your masterpiece, be prepared to take the blame for a left-handed gunslinger wearing a right-handed gun, or a blazing redhead becoming a brunette. One of Christina Dodd's books has turned into a collector's item because it shows a hero and heroine seated on a hill in front of a beautiful castle, and she has three arms—one reaching for her loved one's hand, one propping her into a seated position on the side of the hill and one curling daintily in her lap.

Final Steps to Becoming a Book
After all this, the publicity department takes a look and, perhaps, sends page proofs or advance reading copies (galleys) to trade publications for review.

Meanwhile, the sales department seeks orders.

The printing type is chosen, usually one of twelve different sizes, depending upon the amount of words in the story and the cost of paper. In category romances, it depends upon your word count coming out to however many pages are supposed to be in each book.

Then the book is printed and bound.

Now you know how your manuscript becomes a book. Next, let's look at what's happening to you, the writer, while all that's taking place.

Getting the Call, Getting the Money

So, you've written your book and sent it to the perfect publisher. What happens next?

1. You receive a phone call from an editor who says she wants to buy your story. She has a few things that need to be changed, but she loves your writing. Peel yourself off the ceiling and listen carefully to some of the contract details. She'll go over the advance amount, option clause (which means first acceptance or refusal rights on the next story of the same type that you write), how many books you'll get for free and what percentage of the cover price you'll get as payment. You agree and/or let her know you have just chosen an agent, who your agent is and that you are thrilled. When you hang up the phone, you promptly discover you have holes in your memory and can't recall half of what she said, but at least you know she loves your writing!

Note: Verbal agreements are binding! Whatever you agree to in this phone call pretty much sticks. Therefore, it is a good idea to tell the editor, "Thank you. I'm really thrilled. Let me think about it and call you back tomorrow." Don't worry, the editor's not going to withdraw the offer if you hesitate. Give yourself a chance to think it over, perhaps find an agent or get some advice from your published friends. (Finding an agent once you have an offer is usually pretty easy, even if none of them would touch you beforehand.)

2. Three to six weeks later, you receive a contract, usually in triplicate, in which you sign every page. In that contract you agree to

the terms you already agreed to verbally over the phone. After signing, send back all copies to the publisher or agent.

3. About four weeks later, you'll get half of your advance along with your copy of the contract, now also signed by the house representative.

4. The other half of the monies will be forthcoming when you've completed the book and the editor has okayed whatever changes or revisions you were asked to make. Once your manuscript is accepted, look for the other half of the advance check to arrive within four to six weeks.

5. A line-edited copy of your story will arrive and you will get to read all the changes the editors made. Or not. It's a copy of your story with all kinds of comments. It hurts, it feels strange, it feels good when you find pages with nothing written on them. Most of all, it's a learning tool for the next book.

6. Just before the book is printed, you receive galleys—the exact prototype of your story the way it will be printed en masse. *Read it carefully!* Paragraphs can get deleted that neither the editor nor you eliminated. Computers are strange animals.

7. A month or more before your book is due to hit the stands, you should receive your very own copies, along with copies of your cover. (Frame the cover and keep it over your desk for the next one. It's inspiring. And, yes, you can do it again. Honest.)

8. From that point on, you'll be paid with *royalties*. Each publishing house has a different semiannual schedule for paying royalties (March/September or May/November, etc.), which will be stated in your contract. Your agent, if you have one, will verify it. Royalty statements will begin arriving within three to six months after your book is printed. That statement will subtract your advance and show how many copies were sold and how many languages your book is printed in.

Your publishing company will *not* show you how much money they withhold from sales for returns. Yes, returns. The publisher guarantees that booksellers and warehouse distributors can return books for full credit if they are not sold. If it's a paperback, the store can strip the front cover off the book and send in only the cover. It takes time to get this straightened out, so the withholding goes on for years. Sometimes a company will withhold 75 percent on the first royalty statement, 60 percent on the second statement, 50 percent on the next and so forth.

Sometimes, books are finally through with this type of bookkeeping in four or five years. Sometimes they're not. . . .

The Distributor

What happens to your book when it leaves the publisher? It goes to that very important entity: the *distributor*. Also known as *wholesalers*, distributors are a bookseller's best friend because they maintain just-in-time inventory. The bookstore seller counts on fast delivery of hot products and best-sellers. Because the wholesaler has a warehouse, the bookstore doesn't need extra backroom space for stocking.

Small, independent bookstores depend upon wholesalers to get them the books they need when they need them. Some stores, too small to see most publishers' representatives, buy directly from the wholesaler who furnishes catalogs with descriptions of key titles.

The book sales of authors on friendly terms with a wholesaler sometimes make a difference in royalty statements. If a wholesaler likes the author's work, this is a side of promotion that should not be overlooked. An author wishing to promote his work should include the local wholesaler as part of publicizing the book. The wholesale buyers must first purchase your book, so make sure you write them about your title three or four months prior to publication. They will place your letter with the publisher's kit and hopefully use it when it's time to buy.

When the book arrives, call your publisher and find out where the distribution center is in your area. If you're uncertain about the editor's information or you live in a major area, ask your local independent booksellers or other writers. Visit the distribution or wholesaler office center, and sign and sticker all of your copies. Advertise in the product catalogs or mailings, and give teasers about your story to local booksellers so they will order more of your work. While you're at it, take doughnuts and hot coffee to the drivers around 5 A.M. in the morning when they're distributing your books to the stores. They work hard.

Next: the final step in getting your book into the hands of the readers.

You can't write a romance for the money, because writing romance for the money is a cynical attitude and cynics don't make it in this business.
—Vicki Lewis Thompson

The Bookseller

Make friends with your local booksellers—especially the independents, whose close interaction with loyal and avid readers is a definite advantage. Small, independent bookstore owners are always readers who advise customers on the best in the genre of their interest. Some independents are known as mystery bookstores because the owner is most interested in that type of book. Others are known as romance stores because therein lies the owner's interest. Many are just plain genre stores: They carry all the genres and someone volunteers to keep books in order to feed their voracious reading habit. Usually, the owner of an independent bookstore also works there. A lot. And their hired salespeople are also avid readers.

Large bookstores also try to hire salespeople with a love of books. We can tell you, however, that it's not a requirement for employment in any chain we know. If we had our way, every writer would work in a bookstore for at least three months—during the Christmas rush—to realize the depth and breadth of the industry.

You can lie to your lover, lie to your editor, and for damn sure lie to your mother. But a good writer never lies to her reader. No exceptions.
—*Alison Hart aka Jennifer Green*

In any bookstore, large or small, it is always in the author's best interests to get to know the sales personnel and to keep the bookstore owner/manager informed when you have the publication date of your novel.

What About Agents?

Agents are the salespeople you hire to sell your book—if you can get one to accept the job! Unless you have a track record in publishing, it is hard to get a good agent—but not impossible. You can sell your book without an agent, but with many publishers accepting only agented manuscripts, it is a long, hard road with many hazards.

Rewrite, Rewrite, Rewrite . . . and do it before you show the manuscript to either an agent or an editor. It won't do to defend yourself by saying that it's only a first draft. Show those who might consider buying your book the very best you have.
—*Barbara Delinsky*

What Can an Agent Do for You?

1. An agent knows which publishing houses are looking for your type of manuscript. Without an agent, you could spend valuable weeks, months and even years trying to find a publisher.

2. An agent negotiates the best possible deal for your book contract. After all, if you sell, he makes money too, and his money is based upon how much you get! An agent knows whether contracts for movie, television, electronic and multimedia percentages are fair for you, his client. He knows just how far to go—when to fight and when to give in.

3. If you sell your book and your editor moves to another house or decides to stay home and raise her children, your book is "orphaned." An agent can pull strings to get a qualified editor to handle your work.

4. When your book is produced and sent out to be distributed into bookstores, and you're still waiting for the balance of your advance that was due upon acceptance, your agent will go to bat for you.

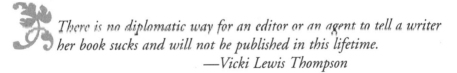

There is no diplomatic way for an editor or an agent to tell a writer her book sucks and will not be published in this lifetime.
—*Vicki Lewis Thompson*

5. An agent will handle foreign publishers and make certain you receive proper remuneration.

6. When your publication date is postponed again and again, and you think you'll never earn royalties, your agent will find the reason and rectify the problem.

7. When your contract says you will receive royalties by a certain date, and a month or more passes without any sign of money, contact your agent. (After all, part of it is his money—usually 15 percent of everything you make.)

8. With publishers cutting back on editorial functions and overworked editors trying to keep up with the political system of their corporate workplace, it is often a good agent who reads, critiques and makes suggestions to her authors before sending the manuscript to a publisher. The publisher counts on this and knows the agent sends only work that is ready to publish.

9. A good agent will try to keep your print run from being less than

31

you were told it would be. And while she can't always keep the publisher from giving you a lousy cover or print so small that it is barely readable, she can be in there pitching for you before and while the book is in production.

10. And when the book is out, but the distribution is so bad that no one can find it, your agent can learn the reason and possibly remedy the situation for the next book.

Remember, an agent is your representative in the publishing world. She knows the procedure and the ethics (the dos and don'ts) of selling you, a talented writer and potential asset to the publisher, through this manuscript and others you will produce in the future.

Before we leave this subject, a warning: Many people who call themselves agents are not legitimate. Often they advertise in writers magazines or show up at writers conferences and conventions. Magazines usually have a disclaimer stating that you answer ads at your own risk. Anyone is allowed to hang a shingle and call themselves an agent. A few so-called agents prey upon hopeful, novice authors to make a fast buck. Usually, they will charge a "reading" fee or will refer you to someone else charging a critique fee. Forget it. They get a percentage of the money aspiring novelists pay for such work.

An honest agent just starting out may advertise for writers, but usually a good agent gets clients by referrals from publishers or published authors.

If you see an agent ad in a writers magazine seeking new writers, go to the library and check the *Literary Market Place* to see if they are members of the Association of Authors' Representatives. Also, if you're a member of Romance Writers of America, call the Houston, Texas office—(281) 440-6885—and ask for a list of reputable agents.

You can also ask the editor for whom you're aiming your book if she recommends any agents. Editors usually have a list of several agents whom the house works with regularly. There is nothing wrong with this system of finding an agent. After all, we all have salespeople, doctors or other professionals that we'd rather work with because we feel comfortable with them.

If you are turned down by agents, don't despair. Just keep writing the best you can while waiting for your break.

If you go to a conference and meet an editor you like, and she requests your work when it is complete, do your best to live up to her expectations. Once you've sold a book, you have a better chance to get a reputable and experienced agent. Yes, this means you can sell your book without an agent; however, it's like wearing two (or three) hats. If your main job is to write books, it's difficult to step out of that role into the corporate world and fight to sell the work you produce. But if you are capable of being professional and businesslike in New York, and you can negotiate contracts in an informed and knowledgeable manner, go for it.

One more thing: Once you have a couple of agents' names, please call or write to let them know you're looking. Talk to them on the phone and see how they respond to your needs.

The agent is one of the most important people in your life; she will handle whatever books she sells *for the rest of your book's life.* Just because you change agents doesn't mean you lose the old one. You don't. Every time you do anything with the book that old agent sold, you have to go through that person.

My all-time best advice was given to me by a sweet, talented editor who had many pearls of wisdom: "Don't rush to an agent. Write a good book and agents will rush to you." Pick your agent carefully and remember that the two of you will be together for a lifetime. There are no true divorces in publishing.

This business will beat you up. It's more about rejection than about success. Even those at the top will still feel the sting of a vicious review, a rotten sell-through or a pass on a manuscript. So you can not let yourself forget the joy—find it in the quiet hours perfecting your craft, in every accomplishment that makes you a better person and a better writer, and in the vibrant community of romance readers and writers. Draw on it—you'll be amazed what it will carry you through.
—Annie Jones aku Natalie Patrick

4 GETTING READY TO WRITE

Finding Information

Once you've chosen the romance line you want to write for, it is very important that you do the following:

1. Contact a Romance Writers of America chapter in your area by calling the Houston office. They'll give you the information on chapters nearest you. Most of the chapters have tip sheets in their files. Or, call the targeted publishing house and ask for their tip sheets on that particular line. Most publishing houses will send tip sheets for romance lines, but not for stand-alone books.

2. If they don't have tip sheets, ask some questions that will help you get started on your project.

    a. What are the word count requirements for that publisher's books? **Answer: For category books, 50,000 to 90,000 words. For large, mainstream books, contemporary or historical, 95,000 to 100,000 words.**

    b. Let's say you want to write a category series romance. Ask the receptionist for the name of the editor in charge of the line for which you've chosen to write. **Answer: Jane Brown**

    c. How many books per month do they publish in that line? (By the way, this question should be known if you've done your homework and visited bookstores.) **Answer: Approximately two per month (twenty-four books per year). Half are from** published authors; the rest are new writers.

d. Is it necessary to be agented to sell to this line? **Answer: Not necessarily, but it would be nice.**

e. Will that editor be attending writers conferences during the year? If so, when and where? **Answer: Only one—in California, July 2.**

f. Does the editor have a favorite book published in her line during the past year? **Answer: Yes.** *Moon Magic* **by Jane Doe.**

Okay, so now you have some answers!

Say this publisher receives at least one thousand queries/manuscripts annually for this line. Because you've done your homework and your writing is as tight as you can make it, your manuscript will be read for one of those twelve slots. (Half are new writers, remember?)

Never say never in the publishing industry. For every instance someone tells you "you can't do this," there is a published example to show that you can indeed do it. The difference is, in your story you have to make it a plausible, integral part of your manuscript.
—*Vickie Moore*

The next step is simply to go for it. After all, we all occasionally play the lottery or bet on a game with a friend. The odds of winning the lottery are around 1,600,000 to 1. The odds of selling a book are much better than that. The publishing industry should have the same slogan the lottery has: If you don't play, you can't win!

So, although it's one in a thousand, it still sounds like pretty good odds to us—especially since you have the drive and determination, or you wouldn't be reading this book. What you need now is more information and the knowledge of how to hone your craft.

What you've just received from this phone call is a lot of information:

- You know the name of the editor.
- You will know the editor's tastes as soon as you get your hands on *Moon Magic*. You can see what specifics she is looking for by analyzing that book.
- You know the house requirements.
- You know what your chances are for selling to that house.

Now, armed with all that knowledge, you have *almost* enough to begin your novel.

35

Setting up a manuscript is like preparing a gourmet meal. Only after you learn to read the recipe, gather up the utensils and lay out the ingredients are you actually ready to cook.
—Diana Whitney

Formatting Your Manuscript

The first rule of publishing: Every manuscript must be double-spaced with a one-inch margin on all sides.

Next, whether you're writing a category or a large, mainstream book, certain standards of manuscript preparation will show your professionalism and make your work easier to read.

Page Headers and First Pages

A *header* is the identification line across the top of the page. It is set up on your computer to repeat the same information at the top of every page of your manuscript. If you don't have a computer, it is necessary to type the header across the top of each page.

A header tells the editor the title, the author's last name and the page number. All page numbers should follow consecutively, meaning if chapter one ends on page 20, chapter two begins on page 21.

It is also helpful, but not required, to put the chapter number or title in the center of the header line. This will help you keep track of where you are when you print out and line edit your manuscript.

When typing your manuscript, remember an editor's eyes get tired. Make it neat and pleasing to the eye.
—Marie Ferrarella

Place your last name next to the page number with about five spaces between it and the number. No slashes! Slashes are jolting and disconcerting to the eye when all the editor wants to know is the page number. However, you want your name close to the number so that every time the editor glances at what page she's on, she sees your name, too.

Page 37 shows what a header looks like.

The editor is the first reader who must be sold on your book. To that end, the first few pages of a manuscript are crucial. They must be physically neat and clean, and intellectually enticing.
—Barbara Delinsky

MOON MAGIC   CHAPTER ONE   DOE   1

WRITE A ROMANCE!   SYNOPSIS   ESTRADA   1

SYNOPSIS

This is the beginning of a *synopsis* or general outline of a story. Notice the heading
and the space skipped down before the text
begins. This format will be followed at the
beginning of every chapter and the synopsis,
as shown.

The synopsis, outline or chapter would continue on from here with the header at the top
of each page, as discussed before.

If you have a computer, format a header with one-inch margins at the top, bottom and sides of your pages. Never justify the right side or margin. Hyphenation breaks up words and makes it difficult to get an accurate word count.

If you are working on a typewriter, leave a one-inch margin at the top and type your header. Then drop down two spaces (i.e., one double space) before beginning your text. Make a template with dark, heavy lines all the way around a one-inch border on a piece of typing paper. Use it under each manuscript page as you type to keep you on course.

Once your header is set up using a computer or typewriter, set the first page of every chapter as shown at the bottom of p. 37. Then drop down two double spaces and begin your story.

Note: When a chapter ends, *never* begin another chapter on the same page. Each new chapter deserves its own set of pages, and you will be trumpeting that you are an amateur if you try to save paper by doing it the other way.

Cover Pages

When your manuscript is complete and ready to go to an editor, make a *cover page*. A cover page goes over the finished manuscript and contains important information about you and your book. See p. 39 for an example of a cover page.

Note: One word of caution: Always use your real name on a manuscript. Your pseudonym can be mentioned on the title page but doesn't need to be, since it will be specified in your contract. Your real name, however, will appear on everything in the editor's file.

Make the Print Readable

Editors read hundreds of manuscripts each month. They will not bother to read faint, barely discernible print from a fading ribbon or cartridge. Therefore, use a new ribbon or ink cartridge when printing the copy of your manuscript you're going to send out.

Don't choose a typeface with small, close-together letters! Use New Courier (first choice), Times New Roman (second choice) or a close match (last choice). The most commonly accepted font size in Courier or Times Roman is 12. Typeface and size is important because editors

```
Mary Smith
11111 Main St.
Apartment #11
Houston, TX 77090
(222)222-2222 home
(333)333-3333 office
(444)444-4444 home fax
yourname@yourisp.com




                        FROM DAWN TO DUSK
                                by
                            MARY SMITH
                            writing as
                            RITA SMITH




        HARLEQUIN TEMPTATION BOOKS           APPROX; 60,000 WORDS
```

and agents read so many manuscripts that they will read only those that are easy on their overworked eyes.

Why Is This Stuff Important?
Knowing the mechanics of manuscript format is important because professional readers/editors will be comparing your manuscript to hun-

isn't formatted correctly, it immediately tells them you are an amateur.

A glance at a stack of manuscripts on a publisher's desk will graphically show which authors are serious about pursuing a writing career. Improper mechanics, haphazard preparation, misspelled words, erasures, white-outs, crossed-out words and phrases, smudged pages, too-thin paper—all make a busy editor disregard or put off reading the manuscript. Occasionally it is trashed or returned unread if the author included postage.

Think of your own job. Don't we all do the easy stuff first, then deal with the harder things? Well, editors have the same pressures and job requirements. It makes sense to follow the basic rules instead of flagrantly disregarding them. When a writer hoping to break into romance writing fails to submit a pristine, correctly formatted work, his manuscript will likely never be read.

All this happens because the writer ignored the most basic criteria for the new profession he wishes to enter and didn't have the courtesy to submit a pristine, correctly formatted manuscript.

Some authors, lacking knowledge of the writing profession, believe their outstanding talent and (in their opinion) brilliant story line will overcome anything lacking in an otherwise sloppy manuscript.

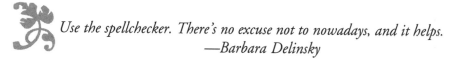

Use the spellchecker. There's no excuse not to nowadays, and it helps.
—Barbara Delinsky

Planning Novel Length

Because the romance industry operates on fairly rigid standards, plan the length of your novel before you write it. This will keep your planned single title from turning out to be 50,000 words too short or your proposed Silhouette Desire 50,000 words too long.

For the sake of simplicity, let's talk about writing a category novel. The first thing you must decide is: How many chapters will your entire manuscript need? Most category lines prefer not less than eight and not more than fourteen chapters in the entire book.

Choose how many chapters you think your book will need to tell the story. Let's say you decide on ten chapters. How many pages will you need for each chapter?

There is a simple way to find the answer to this very important question. Determine how many words you will have on each page. If you use the format we previously described—double-spaced, one-inch margins, New Courier typeface at size 12—you will get an average of 250 words per page.

If you want to write for Harlequin Temptation, for example, you will need 60,000 words to complete a manuscript. Divide 250 average words per page into 60,000, and you get 240 pages. So 240 pages will complete your manuscript.

Now, the last step. Divide the 240 pages by 10, and find the average page count for each chapter: 24 pages to a chapter. That doesn't mean that as you're typing this great scene, you find yourself on page 23 and have to stop. No, ma'am. It means that when you're on page 18 or 19, you know where you're heading, and you know how to plan if you're going to end the chapter with a cliff-hanger. If it takes a few pages more, that's fine. This is probably your first draft and things will change as you reread or readjust. Besides, the only thing truly written in stone is that you turn in the best work of which you're capable.

Note: Be aware that the word count feature on many software programs is not always an accurate way to determine the true length of a manuscript. Publishing houses do it the old-fashioned way, as described above, only they use a much more complicated formula.

How to Submit Your Work

You've produced a complete and salable manuscript for a category book. What do you do now? You get it ready for submission!

Note: All first books must be completed before an editor will look at it. (Everyone wants proof that you can complete a novel before they buy it!) After your first sale, you can sell *on proposal*, which means a synopsis and usually three chapters are all you will need.

You need a lot of heart and a lot of skill; without the heart you can't get the skill.
— *Tess Farraday*

Sending the Manuscript

If your query letter receives a positive response asking to see the work, do the following:

1. Place a cover letter on top of the manuscript referring to the phone call or letter you just received. It is very important to let whomever opens the mail know that this is a requested manuscript, or it will end up in the dreaded slush pile.
2. Put a rubber band around the middle of the manuscript and the letter, with another one from top to bottom.
3. Place it in a large, padded envelope.
4. Before sealing and addressing it, add another large, padded envelope with your return address and sufficient return postage in case the editor turns it down.

Note: Manuscripts are rejected for many reasons—and it's not necessarily the author's fault. It could be something as simple as the editor just bought a story similar to yours. So if the manuscript is returned, send it to another publisher who may be able to look more kindly at it.

Also Note: If the editor has included a note with suggestions for making it better, by all means take those suggestions to heart—and make those revisions! If she has asked to see it again after the revisions are made, *send it back*. Don't delay!

5 'DEM BONES, 'DEM BONES: THE SKELETON OF THE STORY

In archery—as in life and writing—if you don't aim at anything in particular, don't plan on hitting anything in particular either. In other words, before you begin your story, have in your mind the clear, all-important structure. Imagine this as a skeleton standing straight and tall—the better the bone structure, the better the story. A clean skeleton with strong bones will not weaken or break under all the conflicts and disasters your character will face on the way to the story goal. If you know every aspect of this skeleton, you can properly gauge how much stress and when to place it in each individual joint, or scene.

All stories, no matter what genre, have the same skeleton. Every salable book—romance, mystery, western, science fiction, techno-thriller or even a children's book—is built on the same basic foundation. This underlying framework will draw the reader like a magnet and keep him pinned to each page of the book all the way to the end.

All stories supply the following: opening, goal, beginning conflict, continuous conflict on way to goal, big disaster, dark period. Then, lo and behold: resolution (which can be ordinary man becomes superman and wins or loses, but it's still resolved)!

Subplots woven through pages make the difference in the story, but not a difference in the basic, sound structure.

Look at it this way: Despite differences in race, creed and color (all exterior items), all humans have the same basic skeleton and brain cavity (all important, inside items). The only skeletal difference is that some are tall, others are short. Some are male, others are female. End of difference.

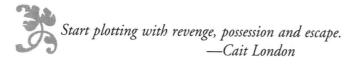 *Believe in yourself and in your own voice, because there will be times in this business when you will be the only one who does. Take heart from the knowledge that an author with a strong voice will often have trouble at the start of his or her career because strong, distinctive voices sometimes make editors nervous. But in the end, only the strong survive. Readers return time and again to the unique, the distinctive, storytelling voice. They may love it or they may hate it, but they do not forget it.*
—Jayne Ann Krentz aka Amanda Quick

Later, after we've given the nuts and bolts of building that framework, we'll talk about *fleshing out* the skeleton—or what makes each person (or character) uniquely different.

The Story's Backbone

Let's begin building the foundation of your story. Start with the *spine* or *backbone* of your book. The backbone is the weaving of two important parts of the structure—the premise and the plot—into one cohesive spine.

Start plotting with revenge, possession and escape.
—Cait London

As stated in chapter one, the premise (reason for your story) is the first step to plotting. Ask yourself: "What am I trying to prove by writing this story?"

Are you trying to prove that a single woman can be a good mother, excel in her career and still find love? Or that an unjustly accused man can fight and win his freedom? Or that an abused child can grow up to be a productive and loving adult?

If you can condense your premise (and plot) into one sentence, you have begun a blueprint for the story. Look at your local television guide. See how they come up with a premise for a television show in one sentence? Do the same, and you can keep your own story on target.

In *The Ivory Key*, (the ghost story mentioned earlier), Rita Clay

Estrada had a three-sentence premise line that stayed above her computer all through the writing.

> He was a man from the past. She was a woman of the present. Together they had no future.

It kept her on target the entire time she wrote!

Not only should every book have a beginning, middle and end, but so should every chapter and every scene.
—*Alina Adams*

Another of Rita's books, *The Will and the Way*, had a different premise: She'd rather be a mistress than a Mrs. Rita kept with that until the heroine realized what she really wanted was what she hadn't wanted before: marriage. A slight twist. Romance, remember? No matter what the goal, in the end she gets what she wants *and* finds love.

In today's story world, romance is not a heroine's goal. She's focused on something else: a child, a trip around the world, her own business or maybe just day-to-day survival. Whatever it is, she usually gets it *and* love, or she finds that her original goal was not really what she wanted.

Show Goal Through Action

The next thing to do after writing the premise of the story—using the previous case of the single mother—is:

1. Plunge right in at the beginning. Show her aiming for her goal, which is the last word in your sentence. She wants a *career*. Do this in speech or thought exhibited through action.
2. How to do this? Show her at her job. Perhaps she's trying to leave work to meet her child. Or leaving her child to get to her job. Harried, waiting for a raise. Whatever way you see someone in this frame of mind will work. Show action immediately.

Have her joy tempered by the fact that she must again leave her child in the care of others. Subtly indicate that although she wants her promotion, she is tired of trying to be mother, father and breadwinner. Mingle hope and despair in her dream of career, especially when she attempts to fit in dating. All this until she falls in love with a man who doesn't fit into her schedule.

Do the same thing in the story of the man unjustly accused.

Again, the first thing to do is plunge right in at the beginning: Show him aiming for his goal, exhibited by the three words in your sentence: *win his freedom.* Add to the end of the premise sentence the words "*and love.*"

Pick him up in jail talking to his attorney about what happened to him. Briefly, let the reader know that he's been unjustly accused. He's lost his wife because of it—and he's yearning for someone who will not only believe he's innocent, but will support him in proving it.

See? From one sentence, you have begun to build the spine, the skeleton of a book.

Now that we've explained premise, let's move on to the action.

Your first chapter contains all the genes necessary for the proper formation of your story.
—*D.J. Resnick*

Why Action Is Important

As in movies and television, a book must have action. And to lure the reader into your story, begin with action.

Twenty or thirty years ago a writer could slowly lead the reader into the story; today, however, we live in a time of instant gratification. Time has speeded up. A reader wants to plunge directly into the story and ride in the skin of a character he enjoys. Through that character, the reader wants to (safely) experience thrilling, dangerous adventures and the wonder of a deep, true love.

Readers want to enjoy the ride through your fantasy and close the book with a feeling of satisfaction. In the end they want to feel gratified for weathering the storms along with the character. And in the process, readers learn how to deal with similar situations—best of all, readers share in the reward.

Beginning your romance story with action pulls the reader straight into the story. What kind of action? Well, definitely not the abuse kind we see so often on television! Remember that a romance novel is about love—the finding of it, the difficulty of adjusting and changing to keep love, and the ultimate reward of love and happiness.

Action at the beginning of a romance novel is any action that sets up the meeting between hero and heroine and sends them into the off-again, on-again dance of love. The action you open your story with depends upon your premise. While the structures of all stories are the same, each has its own unique flavor different from every other. It is up to you, the author, to decide where to begin.

When I once told a new writer she needed more conflict in her book, she protested, "But I don't want my hero and heroine to argue all the time!" She was missing the point. While romantic conflict does come in opposition, a savvy writer knows that in the reader's eyes, passage after passage of petty bickering only jeopardizes the hero's and heroine's "lovability." Thus, a savvy writer will employ other devices such as internal narration, facial expression and humor to show conflict in her dialogue.
—*Adrienne deWolfe*

Remember, a romance novel brings the two main characters together as quickly as possible. All other action influences, changes or endangers the relationship through the feelings and emotions of the hero, heroine or both. That action continues, accelerating and building tension until the two characters, having changed because of it, come together at last in a happily-ever-after ending.

Action Creates Conflict

Chapter one briefly mentioned conflict, but let's expand on it here. First of all, there is no story without conflict. You cannot write about happy people, in a happy house, in a happy town, in a happy country, in a happy world. Why? Because there is no story.

Dwight V. Swain, a master of novel structure, said, "A story tells how a character overcomes obstacles on the way to an important goal."

With all that happiness in that happy house, happy town, happy country and happy world, no obstacles and challenges exist to make the characters fight for a goal, learn in the process and grow.

That's what life—and stories—are all about. For the reader to enter the character and feel hope, love and anguish, there must be basic human emotions, senses, feelings, vices and virtues—all of which are common to humans worldwide. And more than any other genre, a romance novel must address the senses and deep passion regarding love—that most basic emotion that, evident or not, is part of every person on this planet.

In a well-written romance novel, love, hurt, anger, despair and betrayal mingle intermittently with hope; hope is followed by doubt, anticipation followed by desire, fear followed by disloyalty, wishes followed

by faith. The hero and heroine will run the gamut of all these emotions.
"Does she love me?"
"Has he betrayed me?"
"Is she lying?"
"Is he cheating?"

As the conflict of the story continues to build, the hero and heroine, despite all the angst between them, are drawn closer together because their thoughts and emotions are focused on each other.

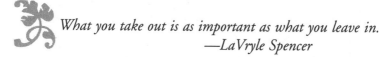

Conflict is the basis of all storytelling. You can write a book with lots of action, but without conflict—within and between the main characters—the action is just so much noise. Repeat after me: Story is conflict.
—Libby Hall writing as Laurie Paige

As in all other genres, action breeds conflict, and conflict is what your story is all about.

The Two Types of Conflict
The two kinds of conflict are:
1. Outer conflict
2. Inner conflict

Outer conflict is an outside event that impacts the main character's life and is something over which she has no control.

Inner conflict is the character's response to that uncontrollable event.

Remember, in a romance novel, the relationship between the hero and heroine is primary. The external plot should be strong enough to affect the love relationship, even if only one of the main characters (hero or heroine) is involved. However, don't make your external conflict so strong that it keeps the hero and heroine separated. Leave room for reconciliation and the ultimate happy ending.

What you take out is as important as what you leave in.
—LaVryle Spencer

The *tempo* or *pacing* of the external conflict reflects upon the internal conflict, which is the character's response to the event—or external plot.

When writing about internal conflict, use feelings, emotions and senses to show the character reaction and the change in perspective each external conflict evokes in the hero or heroine. This constant change through the impact of events also shows how far the character has progressed at each point in time, and builds and adds to character growth.

The external and internal method of plotting (conflict) is also part of the skeleton of your story. It is interwoven with the premise and adds a new dimension to the building or structure of the book.

When writing internal conflict, remember:

1. To have the character (hero or heroine) respond only to the external event that has just happened. Don't have the character react to two or three events at one time.

2. To stay focused mainly on the love story. Don't let an external plot line become greater than the romance.

3. Internal conflict gives the reader insight into the characters on a "gut level." When a reader sees and experiences the character's fears, hopes, dreams and motivation, the hero and heroine are fully exposed. The reader then becomes those characters and lives their lives.

4. The emotional relationship of the characters in a romance novel is often controlled by the external conflict or plot.

5. The outer conflict is most often settled before the inner conflict is resolved. This means that external problems are solved before emotional problems are reconciled. In other words, whatever problems you created between the characters need to be solved before they declare their love and what really kept them apart.

6. Since each external conflict governs the emotional tempo of the lovers, they are usually controlled by the outer plot. The hero/heroine are forced to grow and look, not only at their love partner, but at themselves.

The Narrative Hook

How do you pull the reader into the story in the first place? With the first sentence in the first paragraph on the first page of the book! This is called the *narrative hook*.

Begin your story on the first line. The reader wants to know on the first page why she should read this book. Give her a reason.
—Liz Fielding

49

The narrative hook is a sentence that makes the reader curious about the reason for that sentence. It leads the reader into the next sentence, then the next paragraph, then the next page—until she is so involved with the book that she can't put it down. In a romance novel, the first sentence should hit at the heart of the book: romance!

Examples of a Narrative Hook in a Romance Novel

> When she saw her almost ex-husband and his new girlfriend in the supermarket produce section, Susan Mabry turned abruptly— straight into the arms of a tall, handsome stranger.

Or:

> "I'm sorry, but my ad stated female, not male, to share my house," Joan Evans said, ignoring her instant attraction to the handsome man at her door.

Or:

> She stood alone and lonely under the dim street lamp.

All of these openings plunge readers instantly into action and subtly lead them further into the story.

"What will happen next?" is the question that arises in the readers' minds when you hook them, and if you keep them hooked, they'll follow every word as the tale unfolds.

That question begins the electric connection between character and reader. When you pique the reader's curiosity and make each page a surprising revelation of the interaction between those fictional people, your reader will enter the story and become the character.

Think of your narrative beginning as a fishing hook. When you write the first word of the first paragraph of the first page, you're fishing for readers. Your bait is your ability to entice readers into buying your book. Your fishing pond is every bookstore across the country and all over the world.

Bait, defined, is:

1. The ability to draw a reader into the story and keep him there, page after page, until the end.
2. The honing and perfecting of your talent so that readers will be waiting for whatever you write. In this case, the bait is also the name you will build for yourself through good writing, excellent stories and believable characters.

3. The awareness that your only competition is yourself, because each book you write should be better than the last one.

Throughout all that, realize that in writing, as in every profession, there is a craft—a skill—to be learned. Craftsmanship will accomplish your ultimate goal of becoming and remaining a published author.

When we allow ourselves to be distracted by the outside world, we often fail to "hear" what the characters are trying to tell us.
—Margaret Brownley

You must be a reader if you want to be a writer. If you're studying this book, you have probably been a reader for a long time and have spent much time—and money—in bookstores.

It's hard to be objective about yourself and your personal reason for buying a certain book out of the thousands on the bookshelves.

However, when you walk into a bookstore, look at the browsers. Watch them pick up a book, look at the cover, turn it over and read the blurb on the back, then open the book and turn to the first page.

If your watch has a second hand, see how long it takes before that browser puts the book down and reaches for another. Usually, it's between one and three seconds!

Have you ever wondered why someone picks up book after book and puts them down again before choosing one to buy? Wonder no more. That certain book "hooked" the reader into the character's story; with her curiosity piqued, the reader wants to learn what happens in that fictional world.

Actions don't drive the story. Actions drive emotions, and emotions drive the story.
—Anne Avery

If you fish, you know the importance of having the right equipment, the right bait and the right attitude to catch your quarry.

The equipment is craftsmanship. The bait in a romance novel is an emotional love story. The attitude is *patience*—with yourself and with the time it takes to absorb and properly write a romance.

Putting the Pieces Together

Let's look again at our first example of a narrative hook:

> When she saw her almost ex-husband and his new girlfriend in the supermarket produce section, Susan Mabry turned abruptly— straight into the arms of a tall, handsome stranger.

This sentence opens the book in the middle of action. The action tells the reader four things:

1. **The Problem:** The heroine is still in pain over her separation and pending divorce. Also apparent is that she runs from confrontation. Scarred by her husband's desertion for another woman, she will put up walls against a relationship with another man. This also implies the difficulties the hero and heroine will encounter as they struggle to find happiness.

2. **The Theme:** The first sentence leaves no doubt that this is a romance because the emphasis is on relationship, emotion and situation. Allegorically, the heroine is between two men—the past and the present.

3. **The Heroine:** Without overwriting, her feelings are apparent. The reader is drawn into the heroine through her sense of sight and emotion. Evidently, the scene she views is hurtful because it compels her to turn blindly and abruptly.

4. **The Hero:** How do we know the stranger is the hero? Because he winds up with the heroine in his arms. By the few lines written, we realize it doesn't have to be the hero, but until dialogue is introduced and more is written about him, the reader tends to believe he is the hero.

Bottom line on that first line: ACTION! I open smack dab in the middle of an argument, or a bomb just exploded, or someone just discovered they have a deadly disease . . . something that'll cause reader reaction (eyebrows slamming into hairline, chins banging into chests, frowning, wincing). I want sound effects, too, to go with the facial expressions. Because one thing I don't *want to hear is the noise a book makes when it gets shoved back into the bookstore shelf!*

—Loree Lough

The second example of a narrative hook opened in action:

"I'm sorry, but my ad stated female, not male, to share my house," Joan Evans said, ignoring her instant attraction to the handsome man at her door.

In this case, the opening line was in dialogue, which is always a good way to begin. It also subtly indicated the following:

1. **The Problem:** The heroine is looking for someone to share her home. Finances will usually force a homeowner into this sort of situation. Obviously, she never thought a man might answer her ad. This sentence creates all sorts of possibilities:
   a. She went to great time, expense and work to place the ad, so she must be serious about renting out a portion of her home. Perhaps she will lose her home if she can't find someone to share expenses. Why does she need the money?
   b. Will she allow this stranger to share her home? And if so, why? What is there about him that would make her do that?
   c. If she does, what problems might arise?
2. **The Theme:** The first sentence leaves no doubt that the heroine and hero have a problem. This problem will not be solved by the hero being allowed to remain; the problems have just begun.
3. **The Heroine:** Without overwriting, the reader needs to understand if the heroine placed an ad, she needed someone to share her home and why. Also, the reader feels her problem and is drawn into her through the sense of sight. Who hasn't had money problems at one time or another?
4. **The Hero:** Though we have not yet learned his name, he is the hero because he is the first and only man on the scene. The setup is there to bring them together immediately.

Can you see the possibilities in both stories brought about by a one-sentence narrative hook?

 Never create a situation in which your reader has to assume something.

—Chelley Kitzmiller

Reader Orientation and Reader Satisfaction

We're still at the beginning of your novel, so let's see what is also included in that first paragraph of the first page: reader orientation and reader satisfaction. A successful book supplies both of these immediately.

Reader Orientation

In every scene or event in your book, the reader cannot live the story unless she knows the essential Five "Ws":

Who am I if I enter this story?

Where am I? In what world, country or town is this story set?

What problem am I facing?

When in time is it? Is this a historical or contemporary setting?

Why am I here?

As the reader slides from event into reaction to that event, something happens to the character. The time, place and reason for being there changes. The problem either magnifies, diminishes or disappears, while an entirely different problem (consistent with the main thrust of the story) surfaces.

No matter how dangerous your event, amorous your love scene, or nerve-wracking the impending disaster, the reader can't live it if he isn't grounded into those five Ws.

In real life, whether we face horrific danger, find ourselves in a passionate embrace, or experience heart-wrenching anguish, we never lose contact with our own five "Ws". Knowing *who* we are, *where* we are, *when* in time and *why* we are there allows us to face the *what*: the problem.

Reader Satisfaction

Reader satisfaction means that the story content and the way it flows toward the climax and the resolution are natural and pleasing. The reader feels rewarded for having lived the fantasy.

How is reader satisfaction achieved?

If you base your story on principle—reward the innocent and punish the guilty—you are certain to appeal to the mass-market reader. This also works in a romance novel.

Despite all the bad publicity about "trash" novels by those who never read romance, this genre is well written and more moralistic than most people believe.

Look at it this way:

1. Romance characters are always monogamous and work through family values to do the right thing for child, parents, family and, finally, husband and wife.

2. Romance characters are never perfect. However, their flaws are always forgivable.

3. Love between the hero and heroine smooths away their jagged edges and brings them closer together in a wonderful, lifetime commitment.

We already know the emphasis is on the first of those three points. (If you don't believe that first point is correct, you haven't read enough romances. Go back to the basics and start reading every romance you find.) Let's go directly to point two and talk about those forgivable flaws—the arms and legs of your skeleton. They are controlled and manipulated by the most important part of novel structure: the layered and intertwined premise, plot and conflict spine that hold the story together.

Character Traits Lead to Reader Satisfaction

We touched briefly on character traits when we discussed conflict in chapter one. (See how each portion of novel structure builds upon the other?)

The story about the hamburger-and-beer man and the caviar-and-champagne lady pointed out their differences, which created conflict, and the character traits that had to be modified if the two people were to continue into an enduring relationship.

Traits are the key to plotting. If, at the beginning of your book, you endow a main character with an unforgivable trait—if the hero sneers or hurts a helpless person or animal, or performs a ruthless act—the reader will never forget (or forgive him). No matter how he has changed as the story progresses, the reader will almost always see him as you first introduced him.

True, a hero and heroine should never be perfect. They should have human, understandable vices—as long as they aren't too extreme. And human, understandable characters with opposing traits are what sets up your story line. Their interaction is the reason they come together—to learn from each other and modify that temper, lack of understanding, lack of ability to communicate, etc.

Never give the reader the chance to ask why your character didn't take the logical action. Either explain beforehand or at the time of the incident why there were no other choices. That's called "pointing to the hole."
—*Chelley Kitzmiller*

If you introduce a hero at a ruthless point in his life, give him a plausible reason for having developed that particular rough quality. Maybe he is ruthless toward a man who tried to ruin the company his father spent his life building. However, don't take that ruthlessness into any other part of his life.

If your heroine is bitter about men and indifferent to whether or not she hurts them, give her a good reason. Perhaps she had an abusive father and a brother who, though charming, took her money and anything else he could from her.

In both cases, the hero and heroine could learn something from each other. Their relationship could modify those traits of ruthlessness and bitterness, and by the end of the story, they could be on the road to happiness.

Connecting Characters and Subplot to the Backbone

Subcharacters and Subplots in Long Romance

A big, single-title contemporary romance consists of 100,000 or more words about the main subject: the love and romance between two people.

That relationship is the core of the book. It adds conflict, brings out senses and emotions and is the central force around which all else swirls.

The only purpose for setting, conflict, subcharacters and subplots is to bring two people with opposite views and traits together in a happy ending.

Like a well-made tapestry, any big book blends bold, brash colors with subtle, gentler shades. Now and then a strand of fiery red surprises, startles and evokes strong emotions.

Subcharacters and subplots must never draw more attention than the main characters and the main plot. But unless you can create strong subplots, don't try writing a big, contemporary romance.

Conflict is the key word between hero and heroine, but that is not enough to keep the story going in any big book, historical or contemporary. A subplot should be interwoven with the main conflict to add more friction to the ongoing story. Perhaps an old flame appears at a crucial time in the relationship, or a mother, sister, or brother opposes the lovers. Maybe the hero or heroine has a past, and the townsfolk somehow hear about it. Then the main character has not only a lover to contend with, but the shame and humiliation heaped upon her or him—deserved or not.

In a big, contemporary romance, subcharacters are an important part of the main characters' lives. They exist to present opposite views. If friendly, they do so in an amiable fashion; if not, their views can bring on disaster or hurt the main characters in some way.

Subcharacters are also confidantes. When the heroine pours out her heart to her friend, the reader feels the depth of her love, her hurt and her aspirations. The reader pulls for her to win out over loss.

All characters, main and subcharacters alike, must have clear motivations for their actions. Every person has a perspective unique to his particular personality and position in life. In a big book, subcharacters present a fully rounded picture of the main characters, the story problems and the times in which the story takes place, present or historical.

Connecting Main Characters to the Backbone

In any book, historical or contemporary, the following are vital to gain reader attention and satisfaction:

1. Main characters must be people with whom the reader will empathize and want to enter and become; thus, they will have only slight imperfections. They will change as a result of the conflict, learning to love and care. The characters will grow as the book progresses toward a happy ending.
2. Main characters must be well motivated, aiming toward their chosen goals with all the strength of the personalities the author has designed.
3. Properly designed characters have very distinctive personalities and perspectives.
4. Last but not least: In a big historical or contemporary novel, conflict between the two main characters should be real and diversified, with one resolved conflict leaving room for another. The entire book should never be based upon misunderstanding.

Note: Don't manipulate your characters to do what isn't in their personalities. If you have properly designed your characters, they take on a life of their own and are very different from their creator—with the help of their creator!

Pacing and Characters in the Short Romance

Short contemporary romances run between 55,000 and 90,000 words. These are tightly written, fast-paced stories that are often very sensual. They begin with an idea that can be best presented in a swift, all-engrossing situation involving characters with life problems like those you and your friends may face.

Again, the characters aren't perfect. When their different perspectives and traits create conflict, rough edges are smoothed. As they adjust and readjust to each other, hit them with more conflict to cause each of them to grow or mature. The hero and heroine strive mightily to achieve their goals and dreams.

And, of course, the main theme is romance.

Research: Another Part of the Backbone

We live in modern times. To convince the reader (and editors are readers, too!) to enter and experience your story, build a realistic world by learning how people lived in the time and place you have chosen to write about. When writing a historical, the *flavor* as well as the research of those days must be convincing enough to make the reader put aside reality and enter the illusion you are attempting to portray.

There are three "nevers" to research. Never neglect it. Never rely on someone else's work. And, never let it show.
—Joan Overfield

The ambiance and essence of that time should be evident in setting, character backgrounds and the hurdles they had to conquer to reach their goals.

Even in historical times, people had goals, and they weren't too different from our goals today. Throughout history, people struggled to gain love, health, security, wealth, position, power and a more secure future for their children. Each time period loses or gains some freedoms, gives up old limitations and imposes new restrictions.

The thinking person realizes that, though it may seem distant from our personal lives, history impacts every one of us and the way we interact with others. As it was in the past, it is in the present.

Both historical and contemporary romances often are built around war, religion and politics:

- A man goes off to war.
- A lover becomes a priest (or nun).
- A character becomes a politician (past or present, male or female), giving up honor, love and even integrity to gain power, prestige and wealth.

Think specifically about women's roles and decisions:
- A woman waits for her lover's return from war.
- A woman, despairing of love, becomes the family spinster.
- A woman, caught up in the fervor of helping war wounded, becomes a nurse (a la Florence Nightingale) in historic times. Or, in contemporary times, she becomes an executive, turning her back on traditional female roles. Later, she wonders if she did the right thing.

Understand the times you are writing about, because against that ancient mosaic pattern, your characters are born, and they have to be people of their time. The reader needs to be aware of the societal ills, mores and morals of that period. When characters transgress the era's customs, they'll have all the same emotions that heroines and heroes of any time experience: guilt, fear, anguish. Or, if they feel justified in their actions, they will be angry at being placed in the position of defying the unjust laws of their era.

Research and Copyright Infringement
Several guidelines were created when a major fiction writer was sued for copyright infringement in San Francisco by a nonfiction writer who said her work was copied. The writer was advised to settle for the amount the nonfiction author requested because of the astronomical cost of fighting the case. She agreed to pay until the nonfiction author upped the ante. It went to court, and we all reaped the rewards of the outcome.

The judgment stated that anyone may use nonfiction works for research—indeed, we are supposed to for accuracy—but we cannot use (without quoting) more than three hundred words at a time, or it will be considered copyright infringement. All the other description phrases the nonfiction author considered "hers" were also found in several other books. The fiction author was completely exonerated, but it cost her over $200,000 to do so. Most of us couldn't afford to prove ourselves innocent.

While there are common phrases used in every genre, be careful what you use, and keep the wording as uniquely yours as possible.

Appropriate Feminine Sensibilities
When writing a story set in the past—even the near past—make sure your characters' thoughts and actions fit the times in which they live.

A Regency heroine, for example, would not have today's sensibilities; however, there have been strong (read: headstrong) women fighting for recognition no matter what the period. Women who pushed the barriers to make their ideas known often paid a terrible price. But long after their bodies turned to dust, their acts and spirits were remembered and revered.

Many such women were those who fearlessly stood up to men and told them truths. Women who subtly realized they had power which, when cleverly used, could gain them the man they chose to live with and the way of life they desired.

Remember the old cliches: "Rules were made to be broken." "Nothing ventured, nothing gained."

These women, just like us, had a home to create, men to care for and children to raise. All that, plus their secret dreams they kept hidden from others—sometimes even themselves.

Choose and develop strong, determined women whose impact on strong, determined men creates the conflict necessary to keep the reader reading—and wondering. Will she get her way? Will he see her as not just another woman, but one whose fascination stems from her mind and soul—and her individuality? Will love even the playing field for them both? Or, like other females of her time, will she submit, become his vassal, lose confidence in herself and exist only to do his bidding? But this is only the reader wondering. Your heroine has set her life course. She uses whatever she can to survive and thrive, including feminine wiles (since, until recently, that was a woman's only recourse) to gain the man she wants and the life she craves for herself and her children.

If you want characters to live, give them a life in which to live. In other words, make the reality of their world as believable as you can. Even the most magnificent hero/heroine must have flaws.
—*Sharon Sala aka Dinah McCall*

Appropriate Masculine Sensibilities

For centuries, men have written about and immortalized others who projected the image of power. Strong, virile, dominant masculine personalities forced many a woman to fearfully submit to whatever circumstances were thrust upon her. History and its various societies expected females and males to live up to these images. Most of them never thought about changing it.

Pirates, sailors and adventurers were lusty and heartless when it came to the many women they loved and left in ports all over the world. Other men in cities, towns and hamlets strung from China to England to the rural South, were ruthless in gaining their own ends. They showed their masculinity by being strong-minded, and they ruled their dependents with an iron hand.

In any case, pirate or shopkeeper, they were men of their times. They sincerely believed in the superiority of the male—and the inferiority of the female, who were placed on earth to serve men in all ways. Women were traded for countries, land, homes, positions and children. Men fostered that exchange, and timid women, helpless to change the rules, bowed down to them.

The hero's strong love for this "different" woman will send him questioning, usually in frustration. He, too, will run the gamut of emotion. Fascination can become an obsession for this woman who has unexpectedly captured his heart. He will simultaneously feel puzzlement, confusion, then anger at her audacity to question or disobey his authority.

Don't forget that love, used in today's context, was foreign to most married couples in history. Love was what you did with a mistress. Loving a wife was not unheard of, but it certainly wasn't built into the criteria for marriage. That contract was often a political move, not an action of the heart.

Research Ensures Historical Accuracy

Characters like those we've discussed are perfect for creating conflict. Remember, though, that even as there are similarities in human progression through the ages, there are also vast disparities between modern and historical times. Every century gives up old freedoms and establishes new ones. They lose old restrictions and levy fresh ones upon their people.

In the nineteenth century, most American men and a few overseas had the freedom to leave town and lose themselves in the "wild" West. A man could easily assume a new identity and dream up a different past with near-certainty that he wouldn't be discovered.

We now live in a computerized century, with social security numbers, driver's licenses, dental records, etc. It is difficult for a person to disappear and turn his back on the past.

For legal testimony endangering a person's life, the Witness Protection Agency produces new ID cards and fictionalizes the person's history. However, if he wants to disappear without legal sanction, he must do the same thing for himself; if the person finds help, he is always in danger because someone else knows what he has done.

The nineteenth century had many "self-made" millionaires. Many men with quick minds, determination and little formal education learned by doing. Faith in themselves and dedication to their dreams let them forge ahead and succeed. They were free to be themselves without government regulations, tax men looking over their shoulders and a restrictive society placing fear in their hearts. They had the liberty to soar as high as their abilities could take them.

Now, at the end of the twentieth century, that freedom is all but gone. Education, degrees and diplomas signify a person's worthiness to hold even the most menial job.

Once, businesses were started with what was called a "shoestring"—and they succeeded. Now, intimidated by society's oft-repeated notion that even a small business takes thousands of dollars to begin, budding entrepreneurs fear even trying.

Up to the end of the nineteenth century, lack of communication and slow travel took its toll on many lives and loves. These restrictions make for very different, poignant stories. For example, those whose family and friends traveled West in covered wagons could only pray their dear ones were safe from Indians, weather and the myriad dangers of that long trek. Often they were forced to accept that their chances of meeting again were very slim.

Today, telephones, computers and other miracles of the electronic age enable us to keep in constant contact with absent loved ones. We can avert a pending disaster or reach a sick or dying cherished one in record time by plane and automobile. We can contact someone on the other side of the world by phone, whereas in historical eras, personal contact and occasional letters designed the fabric of people's lives.

Carry a small notebook with you at all times or keep a pad and pencil in every room. Better yet, invest in a miniature tape recorder and never leave the house without it. Nothing is quite so fleeting as a good idea.
—Jane Tun

Historically, people's goals were similar, but their means of reaching them was limited.

Love and romance problems and the various ways to overcome them have existed between men and women throughout the ages. In a historical novel, the methods of resolving problems were limited by the time it took to communicate: notes instead of telephones, carriages and horseback riding instead of cars, letters instead of planes or trains. Many a problem would have vanished had the hero reached the heroine in time to avert catastrophe. Wars could have been shortened or avoided altogether if it hadn't taken days or weeks for messengers to bring news.

Misunderstandings between lovers frequently grew to enormous proportions when miles separated them. While heroines waited for answers to a crucial question or prayed for denial to a bit of gossip, love could often fade and die—or a new lover could enter the picture.

Life without rapid transportation and rapid communication makes for very different—and interesting—historical romances.

Researching the Contemporary Novel

These points also apply to contemporary romances. Surprised that a contemporary romance novel would take much research? Don't be! A good novel keeps the reader reading and believing that the novelist knows what she is writing about. When you sell your book, readers all over the country will be paying close attention to your story.

However, if your reader lives in Houston and your heroine sees the Gulf of Mexico from her downtown office window, that reader will never again believe anything you write.

Or, if your heroine is in New York City's Plaza Hotel, there is no way she can see Ellis Island in the distance. If she grows grapes for wine, runs a restaurant or owns her own business—do your homework. Research it.

If you're writing about a golf pro, a fashion designer, a model or an architect, research enough of those professions to make your story plausible. Use only the research that applies to your story and convinces the reader that your hero and heroine are knowledgeable about their profession. In other words, make sure your character breathes and is well rounded. (The best advice I received was that it takes 100 percent knowledge of the research to use the 10 percent you need to write it well.)

Save Your Research

Your book is written and you've sent it off. Don't wait by the phone for the editor's call. Instead, clean off your desk and begin the story that's been simmering in the back of your brain for half of the last book. You've even gathered snippets of scenes for it.

But wait!

Take everything you have from the completed manuscript and a copy of every piece of research—brochures, phone numbers and names of people you spoke to—and place it in a box. (A writer friend of mine uses a magazine holder for each book written and sets it on a bookshelf in her office.) Seal it and put it with books you've completed. With that information, there should be a copy of every piece of research you ever did on that book.

You never know when you'll be called and asked about it, so be ready. Have it all in one place that you can go to and immediately verify. "Yes, I know where that town is on that coastline, and the hotel is really in place of a bed and breakfast."

Or: "Yes, they really did film that movie in that small town and the set is still there."

This is important, professional and necessary.

6 GETTING 'EM MOTIVATED

Laurel Thatcher Ulrich once said, "Well-behaved women seldom make history." This is especially true in building a heroine, since it implies that the woman who behaves already knows the rules. She acknowledges that she can either follow them and remain static or break them and become notorious. You must know what you're doing before you can make a solid, educated decision not to do it anymore—whether it's gnashing your teeth, lighting cigarettes or breaking rules. You decide whether to remain on course or break the rules.

> *To create realistic characters, you have to live with them, talk with them, eat with them and dream with them. You'll know you have done this if, when you write the words THE END, you feel like you just said goodbye to your best friends.*
>
> *—Annie Jones aka Natalie Patrick*

Ulrich's quote also refers to your character's thoughts, words and deeds. A character who always follows the rules is probably the most boring character you've *never* read. An editor doesn't want to buy that story because that's a boring character and subsequently, a boring read.

However, taking a character from that comfy, logical, penned-in place to a wild, outrageous or just plain tired-of-it rebellion—now, *that's* an interesting character! Characters come from either end of the

65

spectrum, but very seldom stand in the middle of it.

So what made your heroine go from middle boring to either-side-of-the-spectrum interesting? Why did she decide to change? What made her break rules that she, herself, established or agreed to accept? And what rules were they?

Know Your Characters' Inner Worlds

While we interact with people and the world, 80 percent of our time is spent internally with our thinking, evaluating selves. All that happens in the world around us is assimilated into this inner world, where it is sorted and sifted, filed or discarded.

Feelings, senses and emotions also swirl around in this mix; these same concerns should swirl around inside our characters, too. Questions like:

- How will this move affect me and my life?
- What did he mean by that statement?
- Is she whispering about me?
- I thought he loved me, but he's flirting with another girl.
- How will the reorganization of the company affect my job?

All that internalization is what makes each person unique. It's the head—or skull, if you'd rather—of the skeleton. It's the place where feelings and emotions live, where character traits, motivations and decisions reside—the soul of the character.

Life gets painful at times. When the events get me down, one thought pops into mind: "Anything that hurts this much must have a book in it somewhere."

—Jane Bierce

The interior thoughts, feelings and emotions flesh out the skeleton to make a complete, living character. It's what goes on inside your character that is important: the reactions to events, feelings and emotions that make your character spring to life before the eyes of your reader.

Motivation

Motivation is the backbone of every character. Emotion is the reflex to motivation and is used to underline your characters' flaws, traits and strengths. Pick a motivation and make it the heroine's cause.

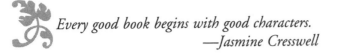

Every good book begins with good characters.
—Jasmine Cresswell

Motivation is the reason a character acts, struggles and attempts to achieve. Some examples are:

- A strong sense of justice motivates your heroine to fight injustice.
- A remembered betrayal prevents your hero from trusting people.
- The memory of childhood poverty motivates your heroine to help others out of it.

An otherwise passive character will spring into action when a situation triggers strong emotions from the past or stands in the way of an important goal. For example, when your hero sees another person rendered helpless or taken advantage of, he will either help the person or turn away—and since he's your hero, he'll help. (If he turns away, he'd better have a very strong motivation for doing so, or the reader will cease to see him as a hero.)

Motivation makes your character do something to change that situation, help another character and *act*. It drives your characters to set goals; in so doing, they become human to the reader. Motivation is something every major character in your book must have—a reason for doing what they do.

Successful dialogue is not forcing the characters to say what you want them to say. It's getting them to say what they must say *in order to survive.*

—Havens, Playwright

The prime motivators for human behavior are fairly obvious:

Love
Hate
Lust
Fear
Jealousy
Revenge
Greed
Power

These are the strongest motivators and have driven characters to action countless times. While they can still be used countless more times, be careful to keep your characters' motivations original, not trite or clichéd.

Motivations From the Past

The life history you give your characters will decide the way they react to the events in your story. Remember, no two people have the same perspective—that's why three people will give different reports on the same accident. Everyone has a different background and a different way of looking at things. Usually, those differences are rooted in their past.

When designing your characters, give them a past—a background that shaped who they are when the story begins. For example, the oldest child in a large family will have a different outlook on life than the baby of the family. Likewise, an abused child will have a different perspective than one who was loved and cherished during childhood.

Characterization is a daunting word, but in reality, it's merely a means of creating the girl next door or the guy down the street. You give her all your good qualities plus a few you wish you had, and add a manageable flaw. Him, you can just give some brains, then let him mow the lawn bare-chested so he can show his intriguingly rough edges.
—Faye Ashley aka Ashley Summers

You don't have to go into a long background story; especially in a category book, there isn't room for this. The purpose of character background is to help design the traits that will impact the character's life for good or evil.

The traits of the oldest child in a family will depend on whether the family was nurturing or expected her to be nursemaid/houseworker. Here are two examples of the different traits an oldest child may have:

Oldest Child Nursemaid/Worker	Nurtured Oldest Child
Resentful	Good natured
Dislikes children	Loves children
Dislikes taking orders	Obedient
Wary/mistrustful	Pliant/trusting

Look at these two different characters. Which one would you choose for a book? Who do you think would be most interesting? If you said the Nursemaid/Worker, good choice!

Find out what your character wants more than anything in the world, then make it impossible for them to get (till the end).
—*Alina Adams*

A good-natured character—pliant, trusting and obedient—makes for a very dull story. No stressful life experience from the character's past exists to create conflict in the present story. Stress and the struggle toward a goal gives a character life and strength. It brings out the best in real people, as well as in fictional characters.

The story of a woman who, as the oldest child in her family, was forced to play nursemaid and houseworker will be interesting because each of those resentful traits began in her childhood. What she experiences as an adult will modify or change those traits in some way. Children moving in, around and through the character's daily life will give her a new perspective about those little people. And to earn a living, the character must learn to do the bidding of her boss.

To interact with and eventually love the hero, the heroine's resentment must be tempered by the events of the story. Those initial traits will slowly change as the story progresses and the hero and heroine meet. The heroine will gain a new perspective, and the story will thus flow into the happy ending essential to every romance novel.

Internal Motivation

Your hero and heroine must be strong inside, whether they know it or not. They must be people who have fought to be themselves, people willing to fight against all odds, or people whose principles won't allow them to fight. In any case, their motivation is what defines them.

You've heard the expression, "Pick your fights." Well, the same is true in writing. Choose something that stirs you *and* stirs the character; then have her—and you, the writer—fight for it. Just make sure that the character you've chosen is becoming larger than life—and believable while doing so.

Pick the names of your characters carefully, you'll be living with them an eternity. Avoid two characters who have names starting with the same letter. It's confusing. Avoid first names that have the same number of syllables as the last name. They rarely sound right. Avoid names that rhyme.
—*Alina Adams*

Stories are everywhere. Presentation determines whether or not a reader will "buy" your premise. You can show anything in the act of becoming by doing something as simple as deciding to cut your character's hair.

> She looked in the mirror and knew it was time. It was a simple matter, really. Her ex-husband had loved it, and now he was gone. There was no sense in hanging on to it or the past anymore.
>
> Suddenly, everything to do with her hair brought him to mind. She hated the time and effort of brushing. It was a reminder that she grew this mop for a man who left her for a sophisticated, high-powered, short-haired co-worker. It had taken her twelve years to grow it so long for him—the length of their courtship and marriage. But it was over. It was time for a change. A drastic change for her, but probably not for a thousand other women out there.
>
> She reached for the thick rope of hair that fell down her back to her rump and brought it over her shoulders to rest against her collarbone to cover her breast. Taking a ponytail holder, she used her shoulder as a guide, and placed the elastic band shoulder-high to hold the hair in a solid lump.
>
> Then, thinking about the consequences of her actions, she held it for one minute more before picking up the scissors and hacking away. In less than five minutes, it was gone. A separate, brown entity hanging lifeless in her tight grip.
>
> She stared into the mirror. She didn't know the woman staring back at her, hair chopped and sticking out all over as if she'd stuck her fingers in a light socket. The wide-eyed image staring at her snapped her back to sanity. Her breath caught in her throat, sounding suspiciously like a sob.
>
> Dear sweet heaven! What had she done?

In this instance, the character was motivated to cut her hair because it was symbolic of a hurtful past she wanted to forget. She had followed the rules until this time. Now, she became defiant; not of the times, but of her ex-husband who wasn't even there.

External Motivation

Let's say you have a heroine who rigidly follows the rules to the nth degree. Boring, right? But what if following the rules gets her in trouble and makes her rude, breaking another one of her rules? In this case, the character might be motivated to action by something external. Perhaps your heroine sees a child steal a candy bar:

"Sir?" Amanda called to the handsome man walking out of the convenience store. A little boy walked quickly beside him, rushing out the door and down the covered walkway. "Uh, sir?" she called again, walking toward them in an effort to gain his attention.

He probably hadn't noticed her standing behind him near the cash register. She wasn't the type to catch the attention of a man like him. But she would, she decided. She wasn't going to let anyone rip off the store's owner, Mr. Song. "You! Sir! The one with the little boy!"

The man stopped just outside the door, then turned, his sharp, blue-eyed gaze finally spotting the woman who had been trying to catch his attention. He frowned. "Are you talking to me?"

"Yes." Amanda stepped out the door and allowed it to close slowly behind her. "I'm sorry to bother you and your son, but, uh," she hesitated. Now that she had his attention, how did she say what she needed to?

"But what?" he asked, his voice holding an edge of impatience.

That did it. If he'd have been kind, she would have disappeared into the woodwork. But not now. Rudeness was never an option for anyone.

She stood tall and looked at him without wavering. "I'm sorry to halt you on your important travels, but your son has a candy bar in his pocket that neither he nor you paid for."

The man's eyes narrowed. "What?"

Amanda refused to back down. "Your son. Right pocket. Candy bar."

The little boy in question looked, fearfully wide-eyed, from her to his father, then back to her.

"And is this any of your business?" the man asked.

"Yes. Mr. Song works long, hard hours to feed and clothe his large family. He's recovering from a heart attack. A stolen candy bar hurts everyone. Especially your son and Mr. Song."

He stared down at the boy sternly. "Is this true?"

The little boy's eyes filmed with tears. He vehemently shook his head, denying her accusation. "Honest, Unca Brad."

The man looked back at Amanda. "He says he didn't take it. You must be mistaken, Miss."

He assumed she wasn't married. That really did it! She wasn't about to back down now. "It's Mrs., and check his pocket, please."

"I don't have to. He says he didn't do it."

"Then you don't believe me?" Amanda asked, her brows rising just as his had.

"No." He turned away and headed toward the deep blue Lexus.

"You're doing your nephew a great disservice by not teaching him to do the right thing," Amanda called after him. "I'll pay Mr. Song for the stolen candy bar, but your nephew owes me sixty-five cents."

He ignored her, slipped the little boy into the back seat and made sure the seat belt was buckled properly. The little guy might be a thief, but he was a safe thief.

Here we took a character who usually follows the rules and made her continue this as avidly as possible. And the engine of that motivation—Mr. Song, who had a heart attack—wasn't even in the scene. You didn't have to meet him or know any more than that he'd been kind to customers. It was enough for her to stand up for him, so you know that your heroine cared.

With the motivation we gave her, the character became a little larger than ordinary life. She broke the rules, which is one of the keys that makes her real. Believable. Honest.

The words spoken by your characters speak to the reader's ears. The words unspoken by your characters speak to the reader's hearts.
—*Jennifer Dunne*

Strength of Purpose

You can see in the first paragraph that each of these characters had a purpose. Character development and strength of purpose are also immediately noticed.

Your characters must have more than the motivation for their behavior inside them; you have to let the reader know where it comes from to make it believable. Give your characters histories and reasons behind their motivations to prove why they act the way they do. Readers must be able to see the implied trait that motivated each of these characters and made them take action—their strength of purpose.

All characters—especially those in a romance novel—must have strong emotions and motivations. That's what a romance is about: the upheaval of emotions brought about by hate, betrayal, conflict and love. All characters, especially the heroine and hero, should have a strength of purpose.

If plot is the train that moves the story down the track in the exact direction you want it to go, then the character is the engine. Without it, everything stalls.

The character is what sells your story—and hers.

The character is what makes the readers believe.

The character must be as real a person as you can make her. You can write anything about her, but she must be a character strong enough to make your readers suspend their disbelief.

You can do this.

Don't create a woman who's strong willed and aggressive in all respects and then have her throw up her hands in defeat at the first sign of trouble, leaving the hero to come to her rescue. Characters become real when they fit the reality of their world.
—*Sharon Sala aka Dinah McCall*

Motivating the Adversary

An *adversary* is the character in a novel whose sole purpose is to place obstacles in the path of the heroine and hero. It is the enemy in whatever form you choose to use. The adversary tests the main character's mettle. As she struggles to overcome the obstacle blocking her goal, the heroine sharpens her innate abilities, learns to dodge and counterpunch (literally and figuratively) and gains insight into a character totally unlike herself. In short, the heroine grows.

An adversary can be many things:

1. **Another person:** a stalker, a hostile Indian trailing a wagon train, a former friend, an ex-girlfriend, a mom, a dad, a boss, a fellow worker, a shopkeeper, etc.
2. **An animal:** a dragon in a medieval tale, a fox in a lair, a shark circling a sinking boat, etc.

3. **Nature:** a weather phenomenon—hurricane, earthquake, forest fire, flood—or a dense woods, a desert, an ocean, etc.
4. **Time:** a race against the clock, a separation of years, etc. Also effective when used in conjunction with any of the previous elements.

Put your characters out on a limb and make them choose. Make those characters work. Learn to balance them, playing them off against each other.

—Cait Logan

When designing a villain, make certain you come up with a worthy adversary. Don't pit a weak adversary against a strong hero or heroine. There isn't a story unless your main character is forced to fight hard for her goal.

Also, make sure an adversary has a darn good reason for going against the main character. The adversary's reason must be as important to him as the main character's goal is to her.

You may wish to use a human adversary—say, a stalker. What is the stalker's motivation? He may be a former lover unwilling to accept that the love affair is over. When he's with the heroine, he feels loved, ordinary and calm, but when he's not, he doesn't think clearly, feels abandoned, feels hatred towards others.

Perhaps the adversary is a Comanche warrior, trailing a wagon train to assess the strength of those guarding it. He knows the train will continue across sacred land, destroying it with camps and wagon tracks. It will destroy the sacred burial grounds if his tribe doesn't stop it.

Whether human, animal or weather, an adversary in a novel must be ongoing so the character can struggle, overcome one attack, struggle again, and learn and grow because of it.

7 THE HERO AND THE HEROINE

Obviously, the focus of your romance is the love that develops between your hero and heroine. Since these are the two people the reader cares most about, make them as interesting, believable and alive as possible. No matter how interesting your plot is, the reader won't stick with it if your characters don't capture her interest.

The Hero

Hero. Just the word tells what he's like. Heroes are larger-than-life men who save the day because it's the right thing to do—even when they don't want to do the right thing. And they don't do it because they're brave. Heck, ma'am, half the time they're just as scared as the next guy—maybe even more so. But, (and this is a must!) they do the right thing anyway!

But what if a hero doesn't do the right thing?

If he doesn't do it initially, he does it eventually. And if he doesn't do it right away, he'll make up for it when he finally does. Whatever obstacles you have set up for him to overcome, the hero conquers them all. Eventually.

Heroes may have character flaws, problems and episodes where they exhibit a lack of understanding. But a hero is strong, true and honest (for the most part). If it's necessary to lie, he does so to protect the heroine, save her life or make her feel better.

Heroes are basically good men with, perhaps, a tiny streak of wickedness. A touch of "bad guy" is necessary if he's to be forever changed by the love of his life. Most romance readers love the bad boy with a heart of gold that ultimately melts when *she* comes into, and finally becomes, his life. That bad boy is in every guy, whether it's an uptight corporate executive with a delightfully wicked sense of humor or a real Hell's Angel with a heart of gold buried under cynicism. Any extreme you can justify will do.

What's funny is that we've all known someone like that. The guy was usually in high school and, from our viewpoint, he was unapproachable. It was rumored that he did more than just kiss on a date, and he did it very well. No matter how grown-up and responsible he becomes in some aspect, another lacks self-discipline or organization.

So Bad, He's Good

Do you remember the boy with a package of unfiltered cigarettes rolled in his T-shirt sleeve? Sometimes his nonchalant black leather jacket and his piercing stare said he'd fight the whole football team if he had to—and there were rumors that he did. Why, this guy was so bad, he bordered on dangerous.

You can't know where your characters are going if you don't know where they've been. Know their past as well as their present.
—Mary Lynn Baxter

Hold that image of the teen bad boy, then take him ten or twenty years into the future, keeping all the big, small, good and bad things that have happened to him during that time. Put him in a suit, construction gear or an airline pilot uniform. You could even have him not working at all, spending time alone in the woods carving, designing, painting or composing. But his attitude is still the same. The one that says, "I'm big, I'm bad and nothing can make me do anything I don't want to do."

That same guy also has a small, vulnerable, loveable side to him that only the heroine or his mother sees—and sometimes even his mom can't see it.

Now, you have a hero. Granted, he's the kind of hero you wouldn't want your daughter to marry. But, since he's *your* hero, you might make him appealing enough that your daughter might want to marry him—and you might, too.

After all, he's capable of great conversation and quick, decisive thinking. He holds appreciation of what he deems your finer points, and occasionally he sees humor in things other men you've known would never see. In other words, he's a great fantasy man. He's better than any man you know because you don't have to live with him for more than four or five hours a day while you write.

Nice, huh?

Now, that doesn't mean you can't have a good guy go bad. That works, too.

Janet Dailey did the first minister hero in category romance, and it's still one of my favorite books. The hero was wise and wonderful and had a great sense of humor about God and women. Other good guys have all had something in common: They are looking for a helpmate. They're not stupid enough to deny what they want in life: home, family, love. How wonderful and refreshing. They are usually wise and sweet—tempted on occasion, but still have a backbone of steel.

Real vs. Fantasy

Since there are no men around my desk to tell me any differently, I'll be blunt. All men have a stubborn streak that makes no sense to most grown-up, adult women. It reeks of childishness when they're trying to make a point.

Take that stubborn streak, give it motivation, add a dash of unpredictability and you have a hero worth reading about with a problem the heroine will eventually figure out. That hero can be bad boy, good boy, uptight man, conservative, liberal. The rest of it doesn't matter. At that base point, all men are alike. To be fair and honest, real-life males' reasoning, motivations and characterizations usually aren't that well organized, but this is fiction.

We read romance novels not for the handsome heroes, not for the steamy love scenes, but for the involvement of the man in the relationship.

—Vicki Lewis Thompson

I bet there isn't a hero's scenario that you can't make work with the right motivation. It's all in the way you handle it. Remember, you're building a character. A true-to-life good guy gets high grades in high school, graduates from college with honors and then gets his heart dumped on, big time. It curdles him. He'll never be the same again. He throws himself into his career. He'll never trust. He's tainted. Bitter. He's turning meaner than a junkyard dog with every woman he meets, until he meets . . . our heroine.

The Heroine

Gone are the days when the heroine waited around for Mr. Right to rescue her. She's too involved in a real life to keep searching for some guy to make her complete. If you're looking for her, Cinderella's plot still lives, but with a different twist. Now, Cinderella isn't waiting on her wicked stepsisters; she's organizing housemaids across the city for better wages and more time off. She's fair, but unwilling to take less than her share. She's assertive but not aggressive. And she's not afraid of being single and living alone. That doesn't mean she's not lonely on occasion; it means she can handle it when she is.

As much as today's Cinderella would like to have a man in her life, she won't compromise by having just *any* man. Notice that the hero is allowed *into her life*—not allowed to run it, unless she wants it so.

The heroine is not always strong, not always sane, not always omniscient, not always wise and all-knowing. But she is each of those things, one at a time, at various times during the story. The heroine is you without the clutter: wise, silly, funny and true. Her emotions are more clearcut than yours, her needs and wants finely outlined. That's what a story is: one part of life without all the side issues muddying up the water.

Remember, your heroine is the vehicle your reader sits in for most of the story. What impacts your heroine, impacts your reader. And since the hero has to be bigger than life to hold the reader's interest and respect, give him an adversary who is his equal.

In the beginning of every romance novel, the heroine and hero play dueling roles. For the hero, the immediate adversary is the heroine because she forces him to see things in a different way. She makes him *feel* a different way. She forces him to—gasp!—change his mind about a lot of things, but mostly about love, life and life's partners. In other words, the heroine forces him to grow up. She will do this no matter what other adversary is in the picture.

She will command respect, touch his heart and be all things to him that are honest and true—even when she's not. Because a heroine will protect those she loves, she may lie or steal, but she will always become clean, true and honest in the end.

She will not cheat on him, break her marriage vows or give up a child without higher motives.

Now that I've said all this, I go back to my original premise: You can do anything you want as long as you give strong motivation for the action.

A Worthy Adversary

If your only worthy adversaries are your heroine and hero, each confrontation between them will end in a win–win solution. Any other worthy adversary will give the good fight but won't win.

An adversary is in every phase of writing. It might be a time bomb, a volcano, a towering inferno, the sea, a deadline or one of a million other threats. In most of these instances, there is also a villain: a rabble-rouser, a druggie, a stubborn old man who won't go along with the program. Captain Hook in *Peter Pan*. The husbands in *The First Wives Club*. The district attorney in any Perry Mason episode.

We read to find out if the hero will win and how tough the battle will be. The satisfaction a reader feels at the end of the novel is as strong as the good fight within the pages.

Honest.

Think of God and the devil. God always has the edge, of course. It isn't until the New Testament that the devil is turned into more than a fallen angel. He becomes a great adversary—almost-but-not-quite equal. You read for God's triumph, but you also read to see just how wickedly creative and truly, deliciously *bad* the devil is. Why, with just one slipup from God or his saints, you could lose your immortal soul and a chance in heaven.

 *A moment of tension requires an economy of words.*
—*LaVryle Spencer*

In the world of heroes and heroines, it's also evenly matched.

Reading lets your mind flirt with danger without the consequences.

Heroine As Adversary

The hero must be or have a worthy adversary. If you choose the heroine for that role, know it's usually in some form of good (heroine) against redemption (hero).

Enter the heroine.

She's capable, kind, loving and in charge of her life—even if she's in a tight spot or at an emotional low when the book opens. She might even need help, but not necessarily the hero's help—unless, of course, he's qualified for the job.

She makes decisions based upon her personal likes and dislikes. His personality fits with hers, his sense of humor is similar, and his interest in maintaining contact with her is imperative.

And—drum roll, please—she is also attracted to him in a physical sense. After all, that's what makes everyone's heart beat faster. It's the dance of life and works for anyone under ninety-five. It's the reason we marry, have children, laugh, cry and stay together. God and nature created this attraction to the opposite sex to insure the continuance of the species.

But woman is an intellectualized animal, especially if she's the heroine. So is the hero. Therefore, they look for more than the average squirrel, bear or even lion would look for in a mate.

And, before you ask, female availability is certainly not enough. God gave humans the ability to reason, and it's your job as a writer to point out those highly evolved reasoning skills in your characters. The heroine must be discriminating, intelligent, independent and have other things to do than play around in the sack.

The Fatal-Flaw Theory

A good friend of mine, who happens to be a psychologist, once told me that everyone looks at their mate, sees love—and one particular fatal flaw. If it wasn't for this one fatal flaw, everyone would be happily mated for the rest of their lives. But this one flaw could drive a person nuts. It can hurt and make the mate feel unwanted, unloved, unhealthy, lonely, mean, etc. You fill in the blanks.

If only he . . .

> . . . wasn't so jealous.
> . . . didn't play golf every weekend.
> . . . would help with the housework.
> . . . stopped smoking.
> . . . stopped drinking.
> . . . didn't control.
> . . . loved me more.
> . . . loved me less.

If that fatal flaw was erased, we would be thrilled, ecstatic, on-top-of-the-world happy for all of three months—at most. And then, being the humans we are, we'd wake up one morning and find *another* fatal flaw that crept up on us when we weren't looking. Funny, it wasn't so bad before, but now, it's so obvious!

And if it wasn't for this one fatal flaw . . .

You get the picture. One fatal flaw has replaced another or has moved up the ladder to the number one position.

Your hero has one fatal flaw, and so does your heroine. How can that be? Aren't these people go-getters, on top of things, ready to right wrongs and fight the bad people?

Well, almost. As much as it hurts me to admit it publicly, I have flaws. My saving grace is that so does everyone else.

But characters are different than you and me. They have clear wants, needs and goals. They will also have clear faults, or at least clear enough for your readers to understand and identify with.

And, although there are exceptions to every rule, there is still one more rule: The heroine's fatal flaw should not be as big as the hero's fatal flaw. In other words, although they both have stuff to learn, he has more to learn than she does. (This is our own theory, and one we adhere to. But not every published author agrees with this idea.)

My goal as a writer isn't to change the world. I'm content to brighten someone's weekend.
—*Debbie Macomber*

For instance, one of our stories was about Brenda, a single mom of three who believed that when the going got tough, all men left. Her fatal flaw was that she distrusted men. She believed that no man could nurture, emotionally or financially, her whole family. As far as she was concerned, they were just overgrown boys. Brenda had no faith in men to do more than earn money—and none of which was ever shared with her or her children.

Leo, the hero, was a guy who didn't know a thing about kids and really had no interest in learning. As a thirty-something successful attorney, he didn't understand that a lack of money meant more than just cutting back on desserts or not going to the movies twice a week. He had never taken care of anything regularly, other than feeding a goldfish. And when it died, he had a one-minute toilet-side funeral and went on his way—Not really training for raising children.

81

Both Leo and Brenda have lessons to learn from each other. They are attracted to each other. They have their own sense of history and a sense of right and wrong. Neither of them are looking for Ms./Mr. Right. They're just living their lives and doing the best they can with the circumstances given them at the beginning of the book. As the story proceeds, their interaction will give them each a broader perspective and make them grow.

You know what the problems are from this example: Brenda doesn't trust men (and, therefore, Leo), and Leo isn't sure what to do with children. Heck, he's not even sure he likes kids, let alone wants to live with them. But as they get to know each other, they fall in love, identify their problem areas and overcome them for the happy-ever-after end of the book.

Does it work? Sure. But we could have given Leo another problem. Instead of not knowing what kids are like, we could have made him someone who lost his own and didn't want to be confronted with what he lost. Or he could have had a short fuse with children. Each one is a fatal flaw attached to a lesson to be learned.

Losing his own child means Leo will not be generous with someone else's living and breathing child. He needs to learn the good points of *this* child and realize that no child can replace another, but comfort can come from all areas.

A short fuse with children means he has a temper that will hurt others. Leo needs to learn that no matter who or what irritates him, he is in charge of his own emotions. He is the only one who can enchant or repel the child—and the heroine—by his actions. Above all, each man is in charge of his actions. The female is *not* responsible for any actions of a hero. If he wins, he wins by his own hand. The same for her. She rescues herself—and occasionally helps him while she does so. Neither can be completely rescued by the other, but the female should *never* be rescued by the male.

Each fatal flaw will determine your character's lessons, which will in turn help support your plot structure and girdle up that sagging middle. This also exposes the characters, talents, good points and flaws.

Character Appearance

A good writer never stops the story to describe character appearance, setting, etc. The challenge then becomes how to write description without stopping the story and going into a long, boring dissertation about her beautiful hair, smiling eyes, inviting lips and curvaceous figure, or his broad chest, muscular arms, warm smile and so on. More often than not, the best way to incorporate these elements is through *action*.

Action is what keeps your reader glued to the pages. One, two or even three brief sentences will sketch the picture. For example.

> Half hidden, he watched from behind a sand dune as Mary Jones stood straight and tall on what she probably thought was a deserted beach. A strong sea wind whipped her shoulder-length red hair and pressed the sheer dress into her rounded bosom, slender hips and long legs. Her expression was sad as she stared out at a freighter making its slow way across the Gulf of Mexico.

In just three sentences, what has the reader learned?
1. Who: The heroine, Mary Jones.
2. Heroine's appearance: Long, red hair, tall and straight with rounded bosom, long legs and slender hips. Her description implies that she is young and lovely.
3. Her mood: Sad.
4. Introduced another character: The hero or a sinister adversary? How does he know her name is Mary Jones? Does he know her—or does he just know about her? He's a nebulous character, but part of an intriguing narrative hook. Will that first sentence make the reader curious enough to read further?
5. Where: A beach on the Gulf of Mexico.

Two of the five Ws we talked about earlier are answered here. The next couple of sentences could easily answer the other three Ws.

WHY is she there?

WHEN is this happening?

And WHAT is her problem?

Try writing this yourself and see what you come up with. If you can write those three Ws in one or two sentences, your story is off and running.

Your answers to those last three Ws drop hints about the back story.

The Back Story

In his book, *Techniques of the Selling Writer*, Dwight V. Swain said: "A good story begins in the middle, retrieves the past and continues to the end."

Jump straight into the middle of the story. Once you have hooked the reader into the "now" (usually after the first chapter or at least after the first scene and sequel), you can go into the back story.

The back-story rules are as follows:

1. Never begin your story with flashback. The reader must first be hooked into the "now" before he'll willingly go with you into the past.
2. The back story is always preceded by something that triggers the memory.
3. A flashback doesn't need to be all of the past.

Let's take the example of the woman on the beach. Built into the last three Ws—when is it, what is the problem and why is she there—is the first intimation of the flashback.

1. *When is it?* A year after her fiance was killed in a helicopter explosion while on his way to his job on a Gulf oil rig.
2. *Why is she there?* Perhaps just a year ago, she and her fiance lay on this beach planning their future; two days later he died in the explosion.
3. *What is her problem?* Perhaps her grief has kept her life on hold since then. Life is bland and has no meaning.

How can you get all that into one sentence?

> She turned from the water and headed for her car, vowing never to return to Galveston and the dark memories that began and ended here a year ago.

In this way, the story "begins in the middle" as Swain said, and it drops a hint of the past by referring to her sadness.

Since we began the story with a sinister hook, sketched the character and hinted at her sadness, we are still in action. We now continue that action. After the scene ends, we can weave the past into her reaction.

8 HE SAID, SHE SAID

Let's talk about dialogue.

Dialogue is all the wit in movies. It's the dumb things we say and the snappy comebacks we *wish* we'd said. It's poignant, soft, romantic, difficult, earth-shattering, devastating—only better.

Dialogue breathes life into stick-figure characters and gives insight into how they think and feel. It tells the story and moves the narrative along through action—yes, dialogue is action.

Well-written dialogue reveals, little by little, what is going on and in what direction the story is moving. At the same time, it moves the story forward, helps the characters interact and makes sure the reader understands the emotions the character is feeling—or not feeling.

Dialogue is one of the main writing tools that, skillfully used, can make your story come alive in scene and in action.

> *Real conversations ramble on with lots of digressions. In fiction, dialogue is conversation that serves a purpose—to increase tension, share information with the reader. In short, to move the plot along.*
> *—Lynn Emery*

Speak, Don't Preach

Most people don't like to be preached at or to, yet that is just what many beginning writers have their characters doing. Their characters sound

> ### The Four Purposes of Dialogue
> 1. Reveal information about character background or back story.
> 2. Increase the tension.
> 3. Move the story forward.
> 4. Show character motivation, growth, perspective, emotion.

like Julia Sugarbaker from *Designing Women*, only not as interesting or exciting. Their dialogue sounds something like this:

> "So, Jill, how is your half-brother doing? You know, the love child your father had after he left your mother and ran off with the hoochie-coochie dancer? Is he well?"

These writers use their characters to preach to the reader, rather than taking the time to weave that information in naturally. The result is that the characters don't sound authentic, and the reader becomes aware of the writing. Her immersion in the story is gone, and she's likely to put the book down. Why? Because she's come to the story to get away from the real world, and if it can't keep her involved, she'll find another story that can.

Never let your reader become aware of the writing. To do that, keep your characters speaking naturally. Don't let them preach.

Keep It Conversational

Proper English is a must when you're writing, even though the average person doesn't use proper English in his everyday speech. We speak casually when we're conversing with friends and relatives, just as we pay close attention to our English when we have to give a speech. Dialogue should mirror casual conversation, not public speaking. Your character won't suddenly begin speaking in stiff, highbrow terms. For example, if your character is speaking to his mother, he won't say:

> "I'm feeling rather ill. My stomach, you know. My physician tells me it's influenza."

Instead, he'll say:

> "Ma, I'm sick. I can't keep anything down, and the doctor says it's probably the flu."

We also talk differently to different people. The same dialogue would sound slightly different when the character is speaking to his boss:

> "Sorry, I can't come to work today. I'm too sick. The doctor says it's the forty-eight-hour flu and if I go to the office, I'll probably infect everyone there."

His last two conversations—one with his mother, the other with his boss—are true to his natural way of speaking. Only the tone is different. When speaking to his mother, the character is a little boy seeking loving sympathy. When speaking to his boss, he's stating facts and implying that it is to his boss's best interest that he remain at home.

Dialogue Reveals Information

Even without narrative, the following exchange tells the reader many things:

> "You want to marry me?"
>
> "Yes, ma'am."
>
> "Why would you want to do that?"
>
> "Because I'm thinkin' we get on well together."
>
> "And that's a basis for a lifetime of wedded bliss?"
>
> "Yes, ma'am."

Even without a description of the characters or their actions, you get a few facts from this conversation. You know which is the man and which is the woman, and you know the man is probably from the American South or West. You can also tell the woman is a little bit resistant to the idea of marrying this man. So you get a bit of characterization and plot, yet the dialogue sounds completely natural and doesn't preach.

Let's see what happens when we mix in a little narrative:

> Angela's hand stilled on the tea pitcher. She stared at the man who sat on her new leather couch as if he owned it himself. As if he already belonged there.
>
> "You want to marry me?"
>
> "Yes, ma'am," he said, his green eyes full of fun and mischief.
>
> He was as handsome as always and twice as unreliable as he used to be. Some things never changed; Rand Martin was one of those things. Her hands shook as she poured tea into a glass and

filled it with ice cubes. She couldn't think of one logical reason for this madness.

With a voice as calm as she could make it under the circumstances, she asked the question that popped into her befuddled mind. "Why would you want to do that?"

"Because I'm thinkin' we get on well together."

She blinked several times, absorbing his words but not really understanding his meaning. "And that's a basis for a lifetime of wedded bliss?"

He looked surprised at her question. "Yes, ma'am."

What's changed? Not the dialogue. But the narrative surrounding the dialogue tells us a bit more about the scene. It's a contemporary setting (note the leather couch and the ice cubes). We know the names of the characters. We know why the woman is resisting the idea of marriage to this man—she's nervous because she's attracted to handsome Rand Martin, despite his unreliability. (Given the fact that this is a romance, we also suspect that Rand isn't as unreliable as she thinks he is, and that she's probably mistaken for thinking he hasn't changed.)

Dialogue Builds Tension

Dialogue can also build tension. Let's take the previous scene a bit further:

She gave a shaky laugh. "You hardly know me."

"Now, darlin', I know you well enough to ask you for your hand," he corrected softly, his voice sounding like thick, warm brandy.

"But you don't *know* me," she repeated. "You don't know anything about me, really."

As he smiled, deep dimples appeared, framing his firm mouth. She was sure his smile charmed the birds from the trees. It drew her, played with her thoughts, teased and tempted the shadowy, forbidden corners of her mind.

As if understanding her need to be closer and her fear to move, he leaned forward, his gaze holding hers. "As I see it, that gives me the next fifty years or so to figure you out."

88

Can you see the tension building? How his goal is clear? He's not going to accept her argument against marriage. In fact, it seems to make him even more determined. And, although tempted, she is still holding a large part of herself back. She is determined to thwart his nonsense, all while playing with the idea in the safety of her private thoughts.

She is intrigued, yet scared, and the tension is intensified because he is pressuring her. His goal is to make her say yes. Her goal is to be known, to be understood by someone special in her life. He seems far more sure than she does that this is the best thing for them, but since we're not in his point of view, we don't know his true motives. Like the heroine, we aren't sure that he really loves her.

And for this scene, anyway, we *shouldn't* know. Another mistake beginning writers make is "head hopping." Don't jump from viewpoint to viewpoint, and head to head while in a scene. One viewpoint per scene is a good rule of thumb. If you want to switch viewpoints, wait until the scene is over, give a space break, then switch.

Think about your favorite scenes in your favorite books, and we'll bet that author was writing from a single point of view for a large block of time.

—*Molly Swanton and Carla Peltonen,*
writing as Lynn Erickson

Is he the one? Is he in love? Is she being hoodwinked by a deliciously sexy con man? We don't know. But more dialogue will give us the answers. More of the characters' actions will tell us how they really feel about the other.

Showing Your Character's Character

Have you ever been fascinated by a beautiful woman, elegantly dressed in a stylish ensemble and wearing precious jewelry? Did you wish with all your heart that you could be like her, only to change your mind as soon as she opened her mouth? Her grammar is sadly lacking or laced with crudities, or what she says is mean and spiteful. Her beauty and elegant style lose their impact, and the ugly side of her is exposed.

On the other hand, think of a plainly dressed, soft-spoken, gentle woman with irregular features and a soothing voice. Her encouraging, uplifting words often help people over rough spots; in time, she becomes more beautiful than even the loveliest fashion model.

Whomever said "the eyes are the windows of the soul," severely underrated the tongue. Words express a character's inner self—her hopes, dreams and attitudes toward life and people.

What people do as they're talking also tells you something about them—the real story of reactions and feelings. In the previous scene, we could have written that the man's eyes were darting around the room, lighting on her Meissen china or Lladro figurines, her mother's antique ring on a chain around her neck. If that were the case, it would be a pretty safe bet that he was interested in her wealth rather than her person. Red flags would go up.

The word *character* means more than *person*; it's the moral code by which each person lives. Some people's moral codes are broader than others, but we all have them, good or bad. With dialogue, you actually show the moral code of your character—or, the *character* of your character. Remember, your characters should always be a little (or a lot) larger than life. They have flaws, strengths and questions, and they often analyze aloud all the moral decisions and judgments they make.

All this gives a character a unique vocabulary and manner of speaking. As every real person is different, so is each character. Think of the people you know and how each of them has certain favorite phrases they tend to use more often than others. Whenever your character speaks, make certain it is from that character's perspective. Use her vocabulary, mannerisms and way of expressing herself.

Dialogue often grows from the conflict between the hero and heroine. It reveals their feelings, thoughts and moral codes, all while moving the plot forward. Therefore, dialogue is one of the most important tools you can use to make a character come to life.

Something that greatly impacted me early on was when a mentor pointed out that men and women speak differently. By judging contests, I often see the sameness in dialogue mistakes made by many beginning writers.

—*Debbi Quattrone aka Debbi Rawlins*

Dialogue Moves the Story

Dialogue moves; it is action. Dialogue creates fast-paced scenes and thrusts the reader into the story. So much can be told about character personality from conversation, and the story itself is more quickly revealed than in long-winded narrative paragraphs explaining the situation. For example:

> "I told you I wasn't anywhere near the shooting." John Brown ran agitated fingers through thick, dark hair.
>
> "How do you know it was a shooting?" the pretty young attorney asked. "When Sgt. White picked you up, he said you were wanted for questioning in a murder. He said nothing about a shooting."
>
> "He said shooting." He looked away from her searching, blue eyes. "Besides, I didn't even know the guy who was killed."
>
> "Perhaps you heard 'shooting' on the news?"
>
> He turned and stared back. "You said it just happened two hours ago. And Sgt. White picked me up at my dentist's office. By the way, how did he know I was there?"
>
> "He got a telephone tip."
>
> John leaned forward, capturing her gaze with his dark, piercing eyes. "Doesn't that tell you something? Maybe Sgt. White is in cahoots with somebody trying to frame me."
>
> "Why would he do that?"
>
> "Because White hates private detectives. Especially *this* private detective."

What have we learned from this conversation?

1. That a character, John Brown, is a private detective being questioned about a murder by another character, a pretty young attorney.
2. That he may or may not be innocent.
3. That Sgt. White may or may not be in cahoots with the real killer.
4. That John has thick, dark hair and piercing dark eyes. And the pretty attorney has blue eyes.

Less than one full page of dialogue saved paragraph after paragraph of narrative explaining the killing, the suspect and the characters involved.

In *Techniques of the Selling Writer*, Dwight V. Swain says that a conversation like this sets up four things: Situation, Character, Objective, Opponent.

SITUATION—A murder has been committed.

CHARACTER—John Brown is a suspect.

OBJECTIVE—(John's) To prove his innocence (although, since he

looked away, he seems to know more than he's telling).
OPPONENT—Sgt. White? An unknown enemy out to frame him?
Or the young lawyer questioning him?

Less Is More

You've probably heard the saying, "Less is more." In dialogue, it's especially true. Your premise will carry further if unhampered by unnecessary verbiage, and the action of the story will move faster and seem more tense and exciting. Fewer words solidify that electric connection between reader and character and hold interest like a magnet until the end of the book.

When writing dialogue, don't use unnecessary words that we commonly use every day:

"Good morning, Mrs. Smith."
"Good morning, Mr. Jones."
"Isn't it a lovely day?"
"Yes, it certainly is."

This dialogue is totally useless. It tells nothing except that Mrs. Smith and Mr. Jones agree it's a lovely day. It doesn't add to or move the story. Their words reveal nothing about their unique situations, the lives they are living, or their perspective about anything that might be important to the story.

But if Mrs. Smith had replied, "No, it isn't. It's a perfectly miserable day," then we know something about her character, or the beginnings of the conflict. Either she's the kind of person for whom *every* day is miserable, or she has a problem that makes this normally lovely day miserable. The reader then begins to wonder how Mr. Jones will impact Mrs. Smith, and vice versa. Why did these two characters meet? What will happen now that their lives have intersected? How will Mr. Jones help her change her attitude and/or solve her problems? Why will he help her? The rest of the scene should hold clues to at least one or two of these answers and pique the reader's interest enough to draw her into the rest of the story.

Knowing When to Cut

Often, once you get two or more characters talking, they don't want to shut up. As a result, you might end up with pages of dialogue that, while witty and well written, don't move the story. One or two instances of this isn't a bad thing. However, if it happens every scene, your train will quickly derail, and your reader will lose interest or become confused.

The hardest, most important thing I ever had to learn as a writer was that the most beautifully crafted words don't mean squat if they don't advance the plot in some way or reveal something about the characters the reader didn't know before. Cutting a line of snappy dialogue or a wonderful description or a whole scene out of your manuscript can be gut wrenching—especially if it's the most lyrical passage you've ever written!—but it's a basic skill every writer needs to learn. Unnecessary words slow the story down and bore the reader.

—*Candace Schuler*

Once you finish the first draft of your novel, carefully look at each scene and trim the excess dialogue (and, while you're at it, look for excess narrative to cut, too). Make sure every word accomplishes one of the four purposes we listed at the beginning of this chapter.

Do that, and you're on your way to giving readers a book *they* can talk about!

9 BEGINNINGS, SAGGING MIDDLES AND ENDS

Save yourself much time, angst and rewriting by taking time to think your story through before you write it. With a well-thought plan, you'll know exactly where you're going and how you're going to get there, which will keep you from backtracking or throwing out written pages because you got off course. You will also be able to heighten the tension as you go, with the realization that you can tweak early scenes to make a later scene even more powerful.

Scenes and Sequels

Your book is not written in chapters—it's written in scenes and sequels. Like a string of pearls, scenes and sequels keep your story on track and moving toward the heroine's goal. Scenes and sequels are part of the glue that holds your story together.

There are three parts to a scene and three parts to a sequel; not one of them can be skipped:

SCENES = ACTION	SEQUELS = REACTION
1. Goal	1. Reaction
2. Conflict	2. Dilemma
3. Disaster	3. Decision

As we said before, the book should begin in *action*. It should also begin with the heroine's goal.

In chapter five, we told the story of the woman who saw her ex-husband shopping with his live-in girlfriend. Her abrupt turnaround into the arms of a stranger said more than twenty words could—that her goal was to escape being hurt.

The second example was about a woman who wanted to share her home. Whatever her reason, you knew that was her story goal immediately.

Story Goal and Scene Goal

There are two goals in the first scene of your book: a story goal and a scene goal.

The *story goal* is the character's ultimate goal that she is aiming for when the book opens.

The *scene goal* is how to overcome the obstacle that has blocked her path to the story goal.

The scene goal will open every scene after the first scene in your book. Once the story and scene goal are established, begin writing conflict.

Conflict is the meat of your story—the heart of the struggle toward a happy ending. We've already discussed conflict in preceding chapters.

Every scene ends in conflict or the foreshadowing of conflict. Not every conflict has to be the size of an atom bomb. It can be something as simple as spilling coffee on a prom dress ten minutes before the character's date arrives. If her scene goal is to show up at the dance with a date to impress her old boyfriend and perhaps win him back, this little disaster will throw her off the track to her goal. That makes it a pretty big disaster to her!

Once that disaster happens and you've explained it through emotion and action in the scene, go straight into the first point in sequel: reaction.

To preserve pacing, think of a book as a gathered skirt. If it's too big at the waist, you don't grab a clump and make a huge gather there. If it's too small, you don't flatten the gathers in one section. You ease the change all the way around. If the length isn't right, do the same with your book. Don't hurry your end or stretch it out. Make the adjustment throughout.
—*Jo Beverley*

What do you think her *reaction* is? Perhaps she is angry at herself or her younger sister for causing the accident. Perhaps she despairs, gives up and tells herself that she doesn't want to go to the old prom anyway. But, as she goes through her reaction, the face of her once-best friend— the girl who now dates her old boyfriend—rises in her mind's eye. Again, anger brings her back to fight for her goal.

However, she is now in a *dilemma*. There is little time to try to remove the stain on this beautiful dress, bought especially to impress the old boyfriend. Should she try? Should she arrive late to the dance and make an entrance? There is no guarantee the stain will come out, she thinks, and her date may not wait for her. If he goes to the prom without her, she knows there's no way she'll go alone. On the other hand, she has a perfectly good dress, one she wore last year to the junior prom. Should she use these ten minutes before her date arrives to change into that? If she does, perhaps her once-best friend will recognize it and giggle and whisper the fact to all her friends.

Thus, the dilemma becomes whether she should try to get the stain out and risk not going at all, or go in the old dress and risk getting laughed at.

Grab the reader with something that sets up the rest of the book, either in tone, setting, time or mood, as simply as possible.
—*Rachelle Morgan*

Once the dilemma is presented, she must make her *decision*. Let's say she decides to change into last year's dress. Don't linger in decision, but jump into the next scene, when she arrives at the prom and all her worst fears come true. Her once-best friend stares at her dress, then whispers and giggles with classmates.

Then you're back into conflict again, and the cycle starts over. This system will insure that your pacing will remain level, build tension and stay on target throughout the story.

Openings

In the opening, the reader doesn't know this wonderful character you created. The reader will first be caught up by the set of circumstances you created for her to learn to care for this story. The opening catches your reader's attention and explains your character's reasons for telling the story. It is the set of circumstances that allows your reader time to "fall into" the story you are creating.

Grab readers in the very first few pages. If your book doesn't hook them fast, they'll close it and find one that does.
—*Barbara Delinsky*

The opening brings up questions and shows character development. That development must continue for the opening to hook and keep the reader's interest, which is the sole purpose of a catchy beginning. Grab the reader while you introduce her to your character, then show the reader the reasons for this character's actions.

Years ago, writers built up to the story, giving description, thoughts and anything else they wanted to unfold the story at their leisure. Then came television, and in less than a half hour, people could see and hear an entire story. These nineteen- to twenty-two-minute stories would have a beginning, middle, end, a story premise that was known within two minutes of opening credits, a moral or lesson to the story and a satisfactory ending. We even had eight to eleven minutes of breaks during that half hour in which to get something to eat, use the ladies room or talk on the phone. And all the while, we watched one program after another.

The best opening lines grab the reader by the throat and yank them, kicking and screaming, straight into the story. The worst opening lines never leave the bookstore.
—*Diana Whitney*

Television changed more than our way of entertaining ourselves; it changed our way of life. As a television audience, we demanded to be entertained and informed within the first minute or two of each program or we would turn the channel to another station that would do so. We knew that, no matter what the problem, everything would be all right by the time the program finished. It was a mini-novel, a slice of life.

Then came remote controls, which sped up the process of channel selection. Because people could change channels without even getting up, they demanded to be caught in the first ten seconds or less of the program. Show titles and credits were entered two to three minutes *after* the beginning of the program because stories had to grab watchers immediately before they clicked the powerful remote.

The phenomenon of television in the mainstream of our lives caused reading to change, too. Today's audience must be captured within the same ten seconds of the book's beginning. Your best chance of instantly snagging the reader's interest is to begin in the middle of the action and create a feeling of immediacy.

Opening lines should raise questions in the reader's mind that makes her turn the page to find the answer.
—Lynn Emery

If you begin your story by describing the scenery, the dress, the house, the car, it had better contain some action or your reader will put your book back on the shelf and pick up someone else's.

A good opening sketches your characters, tells the reader where they are, what's happening and what is the immediate problem. The opening also gives the character's story goal and scene goal. Once reader's know these, they usually want to know how the heroine achieves those goals, and will keep reading until she does.

Sagging Middles

Remember our story train heading full steam toward a great and satisfying ending? Well, there's a mountain ahead called the middle of the book, and you must get the train over that mountain before it can rocket headlong into the station.

What is the steam that will get you to the top of this mountain? *Tension*. Like an equation, the amount of tension equals the number of complications plus the number of big decisions the heroine is forced to make. The more complications and decisions, the higher the tension; the higher the tension, the harder it is for the reader to put your book down until the end, and the more satisfaction the reader feels at the finish.

This is where a strong beginning is vital. If you have a strong beginning, you're getting a running start at the mountain. For example, let's look at the story we began in chapter six.

A young woman sees a small boy take a candy bar from a grocery store. She tells the uncle, but he doesn't believe it. After he goes home, he finds the candy and realizes the boy lied to him. Back they go to the store and the hero makes the young boy pay Mr. Song, the storekeeper. He also finds out where the young woman lives, so he—and his nephew—can apologize. Here you can start adding complications. The easiest way to do that is to ask, "What if?"

- What if the child is from the same school where she teaches?
- What if the hero is from her new place of work? Or owns it?
- What if the child's parents died and left him with an uncle who doesn't know how to deal with kids? And he's failing quickly?
- What if she lost a child of that same age?
- What if she gave up a child who would be that age?
- What if she doesn't want to be reminded of something or someone she lost?
- What if the child has a serious disease and is dying?

Work all this out at the very beginning, before you get caught up in the characters. Make sure your engine has enough fuel to give it the steam needed to get up that mountain.

Finding the Story

My favorite way to find a story I want to tell is to twist a simple plot until it feels right.

Boy meets girl.

Girl has a secret.

Girl keeps secret from boy as they fall in love.

Boy finds out and they part in anger.

Girl loses all.

Boy returns, repentant, to declare what they both knew all along. He loves her.

Girl is now strong enough to turn him down or take him back.

This is a romance, so Girl takes him back as equal partner.

This is not a formula; it's a guide. All books—category/series, genre, mainstream—have a similar structure. Like flour in a cake, this information can be used any way you want, but it must be "added to" in order to make a good story. The kind of stuff you're cooking is up to you, and the choices are almost limitless.

What's above is just the basics. Now, add ingredients in the form of complications, and you make the story more and more unique. The characters, those wonderful people walking in and out of your story, will make it come alive.

It all comes back to motivation. We honestly believe you can make anything in the whole story world happen as long as the motivation is believable.

Yes, a woman can give away a child and still be a heroine. What's her motivation? How about being too poor to give the child she loves what he needs to grow strong and healthy?

Yes, a woman can be divorced. Twice. Why? Looking for a father figure before growing up enough to know that all she needs is belief in herself. Once that is done, she can be ready for a real love in her life.

Yes, a woman can have an affair with a married man. How about a man who doesn't tell her he's married? Or a man whose wife is in a nursing home? Or a man whose wife is dying?

There are so many new plot twists just waiting for a good reason to exist. They'll defend themselves when you give them reason. If they don't, you need to check the motivation you gave those characters for their actions. It must be strong and true. It must be *real*.

Here's the kicker: The character must be less complicated and more reasonable than the average honest-to- goodness, real-life person.

You see, real people don't always have straight, tried-and-true reasons for what they do. They may have more tangled baggage than you know or see. It's up to you, the writer, to clear out the junk and make sure your character is clear-cut and on target.

In real life, the man may love a woman because he's tired of living alone. She can sew, clean, cook and talk to him when he's lonely. His mother died last year and he misses a female element taking care of him. He wasn't raised to be alone and he's not sure how to survive. He'll also have sex when he needs it, and she can cut out the baby-sitting bill. On top of that, she's nice to be around and makes his heart beat faster. It may be reality, but it isn't romance.

In romance, a man may love a woman because she's sweet and kind to his motherless child, and she makes his heart beat faster. The reasons may be the same, but there's much physiological stuff in reality. My suggestion is to work with two or three major reasons. If you bring in the rest of the real-life reasons, it will just muddy the water. With two or three reasons, you've clarified the problem and given your character something to hang his emotions upon for the end where he realizes that only she can give him what he needs to feel alive and loved.

Love Scenes

As you probably know from reading romances, good love scenes involve two things: emotion and more emotion. Each romance line you write for will have varying amounts of love scenes and a varying degree of explicitness in those scenes. No specific amount or degree is "demanded" by the publisher. They may move it or ask for it to be rewritten, but usually it's because the change makes the story flow better, not because it's required in those pages at that time. The line itself tells you how much physical love you need to fulfill that story. The readers who pick up those books expect a certain amount of lovemaking in whatever line they read.

The trouble with life is there's no background music. Hollywood superenhances love scenes by scoring them. You can do the same if you start with good romantic music and let the rhythm of the music pace your love scene's development and intensity.
—*Jeanne Wood*

If you don't like writing heavy love scenes, find another line to write for. Don't expect to sell a lighter (and we don't mean humor) romance to a line that usually has heavy love scenes. You're not only wasting that publishing house's time, but you're wasting your time submitting it where it doesn't fit. Meanwhile, your book could be on the desk of an editor who is just waiting to publish it!

A love scene is one of the most important parts of a romance novel. It shows the female character's intimate vulnerability, a change in the direction of the relationship, growth potential and intense reader satisfaction. Why satisfaction? Because the reader gets to relive and remember that tender time in courtship when emotions were high, fear of losing our new loved one was constant, and tender thoughts of cherishing the woman were highlighted in every male act of courtship. The everyday business of living, raising children and working gets in the way of those memories of what brought us together to begin with. Love stories bring it all back. How wonderful for us to be able to relive those feelings!

We can only tell you three things about love stories, and you already know them because you're an avid reader.

1. Don't describe graphic detail that should be reserved for a doctor's office. Romances are not and have never been about fitting tab A into slot B. We all know about the mechanics already.

2. Remember that women read to relive the emotion of lovemaking—that time when they were treasured beyond belief. When a man thought and showed that his girl meant more to him than breathing; when he couldn't do without her presence, thinking of

her every night, adoring her every morning. After-play is thus as important as foreplay.

3. If there's no emotion and vulnerability—and lots of it—for both female *and* male, then the love isn't there and it becomes a sex act. Ho hum!

The short contemporary romance is all about love—not sex! A love scene is not a sex scene. Graphic portrayals of the physical act of intercourse are as old as time. Everyone in the world knows what that act entails and what body parts are involved. In a romance novel, it's about two people making love. And while their coming together involves physical contact, it is their love, the growing influence and the emotional effect their lovemaking has on these two people that matters. When writing a love scene, concentrate on the character's feelings and emotions, rather than graphic, pornographic depictions of the act itself.

It bears repeating: Characters in a romance novel are monogamous. If one of the main characters decides to flirt, the motivation should somehow involve the hero or heroine. Maybe the hero wants to make the heroine jealous; or, if the hero drags his feet on commitment, the heroine wants to show him she has others to choose from. Monogamous romance characters are true to each other. And in each love scene, make certain the characters respond according to the natures you endowed them with at the beginning of your story.

The first love scene will differ from the last. Especially since, by that time, the relationship has grown, suffered and endured despite the conflict. Each love scene will build in intensity (meaning feelings and emotions) as the story progresses.

If you follow those three rules and read, read, read, I know you've already absorbed what it takes for a great love scene.

Defending Love Scenes

I'm not afraid of writing love scenes. I'd much rather write about sex than dismemberment.

—*Vicki Lewis Thompson*

It cannot be said enough that there is no need to apologize or accept criticism about the love scenes in romances. You don't need to defend romances or the romance genre, either. If anyone is insensitive enough to make fun of them when they know you write romances for a living, they're worth insulting.

Why? Because it doesn't pay to defend something wonderful to someone stupid. Besides, it usually only happens to the largest genre market in publishing—which also happens to be a female market. It seldom happens in other, more manly, genres.

Ian Fleming never apologized for all the crazy equipment he dreams up or the sex machines he turns his spies into.

Louis L'Amour never apologized for every gunfight you knew was going to be between his pages.

Robert A. Heinlein never apologized for all the off-the-wall worlds he created.

Edgar Rice Burroughs never apologized for Tarzan.

Why should you have to apologize for or defend what is an integral part of the genre you chose to write for? You shouldn't. You don't. Instead, just say one of three things:

To a male: You don't read them, do you? It's okay, some men aren't romantic and macho enough to read romances and find out what women are *really* interested in. It's probably why we have so many divorces.

To a woman: If your husband calls them trash, maybe you could educate him enough to change his mind. He needs help to learn why romances are so good.

To anyone: Women deal with the problems of everyday life, and sometimes these books give solutions, hope or temporary relief to their intricate problems. Romances are just like other forms of entertainment—like football.

10 FINISHING TOUCHES

Revisions

Revision is a word most writers dread, but actually should love. Whether you're doing it yourself before you send the manuscript out or doing it for the editor who has sent your story back with instructions on what to do, you are reviewing your work. Relooking. Revisioning what you wrote. It doesn't necessarily mean you're going to change it; it means you're going to look at it anew and clarify it.

The editor has that new vision. She's never read the story before; therefore, her eyes will notice the inconsistencies that your eyes skipped over or your brain filled in while you were reading. It happens a lot when you've read something over and over again—especially when it's something you've *written* over and over again! And that's the cue to lead into our best tip on revisions.

Find a space where you can curl up for a couple of hours without interruption. (We know one writer who checks into a motel for the day!) Now lean back and read your own manuscript as if it's a new book. You've never seen it before; it belongs to someone else. You're just there for a good, entertaining read.

Let your eye—not your brain—tell the story. If your eye reads every word, you've got a good book. But every place your eye skims to "get on to the next good part," you've found a place to revise. The spot you skim is the spot that needs work, a new vision, a little tightening.

The old writer's saw is that writing is 10 percent writing and 90 percent rewriting, especially for the person trying to break into publication. Unfair as it might be, editors are a lot less forgiving of errors in a new writer's manuscript than they are of established writers. They get so many submissions that they actually look for reasons to reject them, if only just to get them off their desk. So take the time to revise. It makes all the difference in the world.

Cut Out the Chaff

The illusion of reality must always be present when you are writing fiction. If you've properly presented your story, the reader will forget the world around her; ironically, however, you will lose the reader if your created world is *too* big.

> *In the course of writing a book, life can throw so many obstacles in your way. As a writer, and as an individual, there are only two choices on how to deal with it: You can let it make you, or break you. You can use these obstacles as a convenient excuse for not succeeding, or you can use them as a stepping stone to crawl up the mountain as you work to achieve your dream. Those two choices boil down to one thing: How bad do you want the dream?*
> —*Vickie Moore*

In real life, we deal with many things going on in different areas of our lives. Yet does anyone want to hear about those things? Not unless he is a therapist; then you have to pay him to listen. Ninety-nine percent of what goes on in the average person's life is deadly boring. Would you want to read a novel with all that boring stuff in it? Of course not!

The first finishing touch for your romance novel, then, is to reread the entire thing and ruthlessly cut out all the chaff. The boring stuff. The long descriptions of the heroine's morning ritual, the hero washing his car, the trips to the grocery store, the endless business meetings—anything that doesn't move the plot forward, raise the tension and give the reader the next vital piece of information.

Remember, editors are looking for an excuse to reject your work. If you bore them, you'll get a rejection letter. So cut the poignant scene where the heroine sits in the windowsill with her cup of tea, looking longingly out into the night. Get straight to the action!

Give enough information so the reader draws the conclusion "you"
want them to, even if that conclusion is wrong!
—Chelley Kitzmiller

A romance novel is made up of one heroine with a goal, one hero with a (usually contradictory) goal, and the romance between the hero and heroine. Therefore, every scene should show the heroine or hero moving towards achieving their goals, encountering an obstacle to their goals, or moving closer together romantically. When revising your romance novel, remember three things:

1. Because of the novel's focus, hone in on events pertaining to the characters' achievement of their goals.
2. Other characters are brought into the story for the sole purpose of furthering or obstructing the main characters' journeys toward their goals.
3. Because the story focuses only on goal achievement, other unrelated events that would normally happen in real life are screened out. Small incidents relating only to goal achievement are magnified and expanded upon.

Writers who claim they never have to rewrite remind me of all those
teenage boys vowing they "respect you for your mind."
—Alison Hart aka Jennifer Green

Create a Time Line

Make a time line as you reread the first draft of your manuscript. Mark down every mention of a time or day; keep a running total of the time span in which your story takes place. For example:

Monday noon: Heroine made appt. for lunch with friend.

Tuesday afternoon: Ran into hero at bookstore. Made date for Friday.

Thursday: Hero sees heroine outside candy factory.

Friday: Date with hero at pizza parlor. He tells her he saw her on Thursday.

Keep the list close by. You'd be surprised how fast you forget! It saves time and trouble with your poor editor, who makes a list, too. And, believe it or not, you'll still make mistakes!

> *Once the manuscript leaves the writer's hands, the writer has no more control over the project. The only control a writer has is in the writing. An author cannot bend the world to her will no matter how much positive thinking or imaging or visualization that she practices. There are many wonderful books that may never get published in today's marketplace, so a writer shouldn't go crazy trying to "think" a book into publication. Just write the best book possible, send it out and move to the next project. Forward motion and rising action characterize not only a well-written novel but also a well-focused career.*
>
> —*Joanne Reeves*

The End

The most important thing to remember about the ending of your novel is this: The end of your last book is when the reader decides whether or not she wants to buy your *next* book.

Before typing those last two words, be certain that you have tied up all loose ends. If the book ends and even one thread is left dangling, the reader will be disappointed and frustrated that you've left unanswered questions in her mind.

When your book is finished, go back through each paragraph, page and chapter to check these important points:

1. Does my story flow easily from one scene into sequel and back into another scene? Are changes and transitions smooth?
2. Are my characters interesting? At the beginning of the book, do they leave room for growth? Are their actions, reactions, speech and decisions consistent with the original characters I designed?
3. Do I have main characters strong enough and motivated enough to aim for their goals?
4. Are my characters masters of their fates—or are they victims of fate?
5. Do I have a natural plot line, given the people it's impacting? Or have I used contrivances to make the story come out the way I want it to?

If your characters are properly drawn, they will help write their own story. If you try to thrust your own responses into their lives, they will become wooden puppets, doing as they're told. Then you end up with a contrived story.

If you've done all the right things and your characters are alive and well, you'll be sorry to leave them when the story is over—and so will the reader. Leaving your readers wanting more is what makes them buy your next book.

Goals are something each writer must set for herself. They are not immovable, like a fence, and may be readjusted. Make one for today, one for every quarter and one for the year. Keep a chart of your goals where you can see them, and cross out your achievements. At the end of the year, I found myself pleasantly surprised at how much I'd accomplished—when the entire 365 days I'd felt like I was swimming in circles and going no place fast!

—Tina Leonard

The Windup

The following worksheet is one of the most fun and useful parts of this book. Make copies for each of the books you're working on, and keep it with your time line. Or you can tailor this list to your needs and use it any way you want. The basis for this is the checklist I started years ago; it has grown and changed ever since.

You can use the worksheet on pp. 109–111 all through the writing of your book. Add to it with each chapter written, and use it to strengthen and keep your story on track.

Keep the worksheet on your computer and fill in the blanks with as much information as you need. Make it expandable in case if you need more space. This isn't the time to scrimp on paper or thoughts. Let your creative mind expand to its fullest. You'll be surprised how much pours out and how neatly your mind connects the dots to a better plot, character and consequently, book.

So now, without further ado. . . .

Story Checklist

Name of story:

Premise:

Story goal:

    Lesson goal:

    Any holidays:

Female character name:

    Any story behind it?

    Physical description:

    Tags:

    Her goal:

    Personality quirk:

    Growth area:

    Her hobby:

    Her career:

Male character name:

    Any story behind it?

    Physical description:

    Tags:

    His goal:

    Personality quirk:

    Growth area:

    His hobby:

    His career:

1. Friend/relative

    Any story behind it?

    Physical description:

    Tags:

Start date:___ / __/__

End date:__/__/__

109

Quirks/habits:

Purpose/goal:

2. Friend/relative

Any story behind it?

Physical description:

Tags:

Quirks/habits:

Purpose/goal:

3. Animals

Type and attributes:

Quirks/habits:

Revelation of conflict during first meeting

Important revelation of conflict during other meetings

(chapter and scene)

Twist of thoughts (**growth**) or awareness scenes

1.

2.

3.

Dark period

Reason for this:

Who brings it about:

Why?

Revelation of right or wrong

Who?

Why?

Adversary other than person:

Overall time line:

Resolution:

Any additional twist:

Miscellaneous points:

Spoke to agent regarding this project on and about:

___/___/___ RE:

___/___/___ RE:

___/___/___ RE:

Sent project to editor on ___/___/___ **by** ___/___/___

Spoke to editor regarding this project on and about:

___/___/___ RE:

___/___/___ RE:

___/___/___ RE:

Misc. details:

11 RESOURCES

One of our most heartfelt sadnesses is to realize there are people who believe that the worst thing to do is help another woman write, and thus grow competition.

When you write a story, you aren't competing against anyone but yourself. If you don't turn in a story good enough to be published, it won't be. It doesn't matter whether there are two hundred or two thousand stories vying for the position. If the industry doesn't have enough books to buy for the year (which has *never* been the case), there is a slim chance they might buy a bad book. Other than that, you'd better durn well grow into a better writer.

Yes, there is always someone to take your place. But without competition, there is no rising standard of quality. No industry gets better by being without competition. Competition in the marketplace keeps you growing, enables you to try new things, read new books and make new friends in different fields.

Romance Writers of America
We founded the Romance Writers of America (RWA) in December 1980, with the following mission:
- To network and share information with other writers in the genre.
- To help romance authors understand the business of writing.
- To bring romance authors in contact with editors and agents.

- To give ready access to the changing tastes of readers and, ultimately, the changing marketplace.
- To give romance authors identity and a respectable voice in publishing.

We believed, then and now, that helping other women is one of the ten most important things women can do—writers or not, published or not. If we cannot help ourselves, we will not be able to help others. When working together, we create miracles. We've seen it happen over and over.

The Price of Success

With each step you take, you'll find yourself that much closer to your goal of publishing. Be aware, however, that there is a price for your success: As you begin to carve out a career in this industry, you will lose many of your old friends.

It's sad, but true. Some won't understand why you want to be alone, writing, instead of with them. Others will be envious of your success, even if they've never wanted to be published themselves. Still others will fret at the "change" in you, though they may not be able to tell you what that change is.

Don't feel too badly when this happens, because those people weren't really your best friends. If they were, they'd be supportive of your efforts and happy for your success. Besides, you will find a whole new group of friends who believe that reading and writing are second only to loving your family.

Out of that new group of friends, two or three will become almost as close to you as sisters. Learn from them and from the information they can share. Enjoy the varied steps of becoming the published author you want to be.

There is a luck factor in getting published. The luck is this: What you happen to know how to write also happens to be what people want to read.

—Susan Elizabeth Phillips

Once you are successful, help others achieve success. You will never be able to pay back the people who helped you, but you can "pay forward" by helping others. It will make you feel wonderful, and you'll experience the joy of finding new friends.

After all is said and done, you may decide that you're a better reader than you are a writer. Even though you haven't been published, you have learned much about one of your favorite hobbies, met some wonderful people and grown as a person along the way. Not bad.

Either way, you're not the woman you were when you started down this path. You've chosen a road less travelled and have changed your life and the lives of those around you just by thinking of writing as a career.

Too drastic a reaction, you say? Not a bit. Everything we do changes or supports our way of thinking. If we attempt something we've never tried before and make progress, we are encouraged to go forward. Each step you take in a new, different direction makes you grow and change.

Soon, you grow into a discerning reader and a beginning writer. Then a *published* writer. Then you realize you are a published writer with lots of friends who are also writers!

Where to Turn for Help

To start you on this journey, we've enclosed a list of organizations and newsletters that might interest you. Call them before sending any materials, since this industry changes and grows so quickly that some of them may not exist anymore or may have changed address.

For those of you online, go to any publishing house page or RomCom or Painted Desert (www.painteddesert.com), and find links to anything you need to know about books and writers.

Writers Organizations

Following is a list of informational/organizational groups that might help you by offering tools to use along the way.

Enjoy!

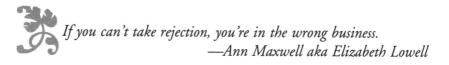

If you can't take rejection, you're in the wrong business.
—*Ann Maxwell aka Elizabeth Lowell*

The Authors Guild, Inc.
330 W. Forty-Second St., 29th Floor
New York, NY 10036-6902
(212) 563-5904

Both published and unpublished writers. Unpublished join as a nonvoting membership. Quarterly newsletter. Call for membership details.

Golden Triangle Writers Guild
4245 Calder Ave.
Beaumont, TX 77706-4628
(409) 898-4894

Organization for published and unpublished. Monthly newsletter. Monthly meetings and annual conference with writing contests for all genres.

Romance Writers of America
3707 FM 1960 West, Suite #555
Houston, TX 77066
(281) 440-6885
Web site: www.rwanational.com

Published and unpublished writers. Informational magazine. Organizational chapter meetings at least once a month. Many chapters in cities across the United States, but also international locations, including Australia and Canada. National Conference as well as small conferences across the country. Call for information packet and chapter nearest you. Also has several suborganizations for published authors of crossover genres. PAN (Published Author Network) for published only.

Novelists Inc. (Ninc)
P.O. Box 1166
Mission, KS 66222
Web site: www.ninc.com

Organization for published authors only. Monthly newsletter. Annual conference held in different areas of country.

Southwest Writers Workshop
1338 Wyoming Blvd. NE, Suite B
Albuquerque, NM 87112-5067

Nonprofit organization for both published and unpublished. Sponsors a conference and contest representing all major writing genres and categories. Monthly newsletter.

Women Writers West
14915 Hamlin St.
Van Nuys, CA 91411-1407

Group of women who meet every month to discuss writing and works in progress.

Writers Publications

Affaire De Coeur
3978 Oak Hill Dr.
Oakland, CA 94605-4931
(510) 569-5675
Web site: www.affairedecoeur.com

Magazine for romance fiction and reviews. Large circulation. Sold in major chain bookstores and through subscriptions.

The Literary Times
P.O. Box 516
Moultonborough, NH 03254
Editor: Diane Potwin
(603) 476-5692
Web site: www.tlt.com

Small quarterly review of romance and author interviews. Available online and through subscriptions.

Paperback Previews
P.O. Box 6781
Albuquerque, NM 87197
(800) 872-4461

Subscription only. Newspaper format. Recent hardcover and paperback books, published with reviews and order blanks to shop by mail. Informative. All recent general fiction and genres. Copy of bestsellers list.

Publishers Weekly
P.O. Box 1979
Marion, OH 43302
(800) 842-1669

The bible of the writing industry. Most libraries subscribe. Holds reviews on every genre including some romance. Inside information on all facets of publishing.

Rendezvous Magazine
1507 Burnham Ave.
Calumet City, IL 60409
(708) 862-9797

Monthly publication by Love Designers Writers Club. Reviews all genres of women's fiction and romance. Also provides market news. Subscription or sold direct by copy.

Romantic Times Magazine
55 Bergen St.
Brooklyn, NY 11201
(718) 237-1097
Web site: www.romantictimes.com

Monthly publication of romance reviews. Also has its own conferences and gossip on writers.

Women's National Book Association
1115 Grandview Dr.
Nashville, TN 37204
(615) 269-1000, ext. 2441
National President: Carolyn T. Wilson

Sponsors educational programs through American Booksellers Association. Also works with American Library Association. Several chapters throughout the United States. Write for brochure.

Writer's Digest
1507 Dana Ave.
Cincinnati, OH 45207
Web site: www.writersdigest.com

Monthly magazine filled with how-to articles written by some of the best names in the industry. Can be subscribed to or bought at major bookstores.

There are more magazines and newsletters out there. Writers conferences usually contain several tables of information and groups to join. One or a hundred are bound to meet your needs.

Postscript

Part of being a writer is having a great imagination. So imagine . . .

You're in your new office. Your computer is waiting to be turned on. You've just sent out your first completed manuscript and are getting ready to write the next novel of your choice. You know better than to wait for word on the first—you're jumping back into writing right away . . . or at least after you cleaned up the messes made by the last novel.

But for this moment, bask in the glow of a project completed and in the mail. You've accomplished something most people only talk about. You've set a goal—several goals—and you're marching toward them, knocking them down one at a time.

It's time to congratulate yourself.

We've just poured the champagne into our fluted crystal glasses. Now, pick it up, raise it in the air and let us salute you.

Our toast is this:

We wish you the ability to fall into your own story as well as those writers' works you have enjoyed.

We wish you the ability to feel the height of great joy, for we know there'll be some new lows you've never thought of before. But joy will outweigh it as long as you remember this is all part of the wonderful journey.

We wish you a new understanding of what makes other people tick, thus understanding yourself and your family even more as the writing days fly by.

We wish you patience to work through the writing problems, just like you work through day-to-day living problems. Both will be solved with or without your manipulation; we know you know that, too.

And most of all, we wish you the friendship of close family, good books, good friends and good feelings.

We wish you adieu . . . and all the best of luck!